T0383934

Cambridge Elements ☰

Elements in Religion and Violence
edited by
James R. Lewis
Wuhan University
Margo Kitts
Hawai`i Pacific University

SACRIFICE

Themes, Theories, and Controversies

Margo Kitts

Hawai`i Pacific University

CAMBRIDGE
UNIVERSITY PRESS

CAMBRIDGE
UNIVERSITY PRESS

University Printing House, Cambridge CB2 8BS, United Kingdom

One Liberty Plaza, 20th Floor, New York, NY 10006, USA

477 Williamstown Road, Port Melbourne, VIC 3207, Australia

314–321, 3rd Floor, Plot 3, Splendor Forum, Jasola District Centre,
New Delhi – 110025, India

103 Penang Road, #05–06/07, Visioncrest Commercial, Singapore 238467

Cambridge University Press is part of the University of Cambridge.

It furthers the University's mission by disseminating knowledge in the pursuit of
education, learning, and research at the highest international levels of excellence.

www.cambridge.org
Information on this title: www.cambridge.org/9781108995511
DOI: 10.1017/9781108997041

First published 2022

A catalogue record for this publication is available from the British Library.

ISBN 978-1-108-99551-1 Paperback
ISSN 2397-9496 (online)
ISSN 2514-3786 (print)

Sacrifice

Themes, Theories, and Controversies

Elements in Religion and Violence

DOI: 10.1017/9781108997041
First published online: July 2022

Margo Kitts
Hawai`i Pacific University

ABSTRACT: After more than a century of grand theorizing about the universal dimensions to the practice of ritual sacrifice, scholars now question the analytical utility of the notion writ large. The word "sacrifice" itself frequently is broken down into its Latin roots, *sacer*, sacred, and *facere*, to do or make – to do or make sacred – which is a huge category and also vague. Presuming it is people and places that are made sacred, we must question the dynamics. Does sacrifice "make sacred" by summoning the presence of gods or ancestors? By offering gifts to them? By dining with them? By restoring or establishing cosmic order? By atoning for personal or collective sins? By rectifying social disequilibrium through scapegoating? By inducing an existential epiphany about life and death? While this short Element cannot cover all complexities and practices, it does treat critically some prominent themes, theories, and controversies concerning sacrifice from ancient to present times.

KEYWORDS: sacrifice, ritual killing, ancient and contemporary sacrificial theories, *Iliad*, Near eastern oath-curses

ISBNs: 9781108995511 (PB), 9781108997041 (OC)
ISSNs: 2397-9496 (online), 2514-3786 (print)

Contents

Introduction

After more than a century of grand theorizing about the universal dimensions to the practice of ritual sacrifice, scholars now question the analytical utility of the notion of sacrifice writ large. The word "sacrifice" itself frequently is broken down into its Latin roots, *sacer*, and *facere*, to do or make sacred – which is a huge category and also vague.[1] Presuming it is people and places that are made sacred, we must question the dynamics. Does sacrifice "make sacred" by summoning the presence of gods or ancestors? By offering gifts to them? By dining with them? By averting their wrath? By atoning for personal or collective sins? By rectifying social disequilibrium through scapegoating? By restoring or establishing cosmic order? By purifying sacred sites? By inducing an existential epiphany about life and death? These are a handful of the diverse models proffered over the past century. Considering that we find accounts of sacrifice on virtually all the world's continents, contextualization of the term and practice will be complex and varied.

One key problem is what kind of acts we should deem sacrificial. Typically, we identify sacrifice with ritual killing, but ritual killing leans far toward the dramatic and doesn't comport well with, for instance, sacrificing soma or ghee to the gods (McClymond 2008). Yet, in the wake of Freud (1918), Girard (1977), and Burkert (1983, 2013), we have learned to consider the ritual killing of animals as trauma-inducing, as generating some kind of ontic seizure – perhaps an *Ergriffenheit* (Jensen 1963[1951]) or *mysterium tremendum* (Otto 1958[1923]). Indeed, it is such epiphanies that reputedly thrust the experience of ritual killing into the religious sphere as opposed simply into the culinary – for example, slaughtering animals and cooking meat.

For comparison, though, as Pongratz-Leisten notes about early Mesopotamian sacrifices, the killing there is less significant than what the

---

[1] See Scheid (2015) on the Latin terminology, including "*rem divinam facere*, 'to make a thing sacred,' often abridged to *facere* ('to sacrifice'), and the etymology of the words designating sacrificial activity, *sacrificare*, *sacrificium* (*sacrum facere*, 'to perform a religious ceremony')."

killing achieves and to what other acts it is attached. Concerning what it achieves, the emphasis is less on the complete annihilation of the victim than on the "transformative, reordering, or reintegrative purposes when [killing is] occurring in a ritually controlled environment" (2012:292). In short, ritual control and larger purpose eclipse the drama of death. Concerning the accompanying acts, in divine offerings the ritual killing might be combined with greeting, kissing, clothing, praying, and singing to the god, which make for a complex of ritualized activities that do not necessarily privilege the killings, which in any case are varied in kind and terminology (Pongratz-Leisten 2007). The point is that one must beware of simple generalizations in the historical study of "sacrificial" rituals.

While we cannot cover all the complexities in this short Element, we can summarize some of the themes, theories, and controversies attached to the topic. First, this Element will sketch two sensational themes that have become impossible to extricate from the study of sacrifice, namely the sweeping trope of patriotic death as sacrifice and remarkable reports of premodern human ritual killings. The first has a vast resonance, particularly in the West, while examples of the latter are restricted, due to the enormous scope of material, to literary reports from the premodern Mesoamerican, Chinese, and Greek milieus, which illustrate the complexity of the subject. Second, it will summarize classical theories of religious sacrifice, touching first on the embryonic theories in biblical, early Christian, Vedic, and classical Greek understandings, then moving on to the nineteenth- and twentieth-century theorists. Third, it will problematize the two typical scenes in the Homeric poems considered to represent sacrifice, *thysia* (commensal) and *horkia/horkos* (oath-making) scenes. These are instructive because they differ hugely in tone, in how they represent the killing and death of the victim, and in their narrative purposes overall. It will be argued that the label sacrifice for these representations from the *Iliad* – one of the earliest literary artifacts of Western culture – is anachronistic and unhelpful for capturing their essences. The Element will conclude by exploring the ritual dynamics of one kind of pan-Near Eastern "sacrifice" that is indeed dedicated to ritual killing. That is oath-sacrifice. Ritual dynamics will be shown to offer a more helpful lens on the subject than the grand sacrificial theories of the past two centuries.

In what follows, readers will notice a preponderance of materials from Western traditions, which can only be explained by the author's restricted field of expertise and the 32,000-word constraint of the Cambridge Elements series. There is also a scarcity of archaeological evidence, which, however fascinating, is simply beyond the introductory purpose of this Element.[2] Ritual theories too are not thoroughly covered, although readers can consult *Elements of Ritual and Violence* (Kitts 2018a) for a summary of those. While it would be fascinating to explore any of these subjects further, this sweep of topics hopefully offers readers an overview of important themes and theories in the field.

1 Themes

The Trope of Patriotic Sacrifice

Probably no term is more resonant in patriotic lore than "sacrifice." Especially in the United States, dying for kin and country is adorned with sacrificial imagery that, if not tied to ritual practices specifically, certainly falls within the sphere of civil religion, as noted by Marvin and Ingle decades ago (1996) and reinvigorated by Bellah (2005) and Gorski (2017), among others. As far back as the Civil War, battlefield deaths could be figured as blood sacrifices and battlefields as "consecrated" by the blood of the fallen (Gorski 2017:98). It is not only wars that attract sacrificial metaphors in US vernacular, but warlike endeavors are particularly rich vehicles for them.

Lest we dismiss these figurations as mere rhetorical flourishes catering uniquely to US tastes, it should be noted that rendering battlefield death as sacrifice permeates the history of Western war rhetoric. Sacrificial imagery permeated the rhetoric of the Great War, for instance (Wintermute 2020), of Western accounts of the Crusades (Gaposchkin 2017:55–62), and of Jewish medieval martyrs' narratives (Shepkaru 2002). Indeed, one can

---

[2] Timothy Insoll provides an archaeological overview (2012) and Dennis Hughes probes the archaeological evidence for ritual killings in chapter 2 of his *Human Sacrifice in Ancient Greece* (1991).

trace it all the way back to Roman *devotio* traditions (Versnel 2015) and even to Pindar fragment 78: "Hear, Alala, daughter of war, prelude of spears, to whom men sacrifice themselves, ... a sacred death."[3] The list could be vastly expanded. Whereas anthropologists and religious historians might prefer to disregard such vernacular as merely metaphorical, as tropes incompatible with reports from fieldwork and with sacrificial theory, the fact that this metaphorical understanding persevered for millennia makes it worth exploring, briefly.

Underpinning the trope of patriotic sacrifice is the notion of noble death, wherein battlefield death is understood not as the mere reduction of human bodies to inert matter but rather as bearing witness to something more pure, sublime, and profound. Droge and Tabor trace the notion of noble death back in classical literature before Eleazer and the mother and sons in 2 and 4 Maccabees, before the figure of Socrates in the *Phaedo*, to the figure of Achilles in the *Iliad* (1992:18). Given the *Iliad*'s status as Western *Ur*-literature, seeding noble death in Homeric epic is plausible,[4] but Droge and Tabor err in attributing Achilles' decision to fight and die to his wholesale purchase of the concept. Achilles dismisses the heroic ethos at *Iliad* 9:318–320 and when he does decide to fight and die, it is not due to a dispassionate stoicism nor to an embrace of beautiful death in battle – granted, an extraordinary theme in the *Iliad*. Rather, his decision is motivated foremost by love, grief, and a desire for revenge, as he eloquently tells his mother at 18:98–104[5] (Kitts 2018b). Achilles aside, though, it cannot be denied that the poem does extol warriors who die beautifully, who fall as

---

[3] ᾇ θύεται ἄνδρες ... τόν ἱερόθυτον θάνατον. Pindar Fragment 78.

[4] N.b., the conversations between Sarpedon and Glaucos at 12:310–328, between Hector and Andromache at 6:440–449.

[5] "Then let me die, since I was unable
to protect my companion who was killed, who perished far from his fatherland,
and he needed me to be his protector.
So now I am not returning to my own fatherland,
since I was no light to Patroclus nor to my other companions,
the many subdued by godlike Hector.
Rather I sat by the ships, a useless burden on the cultivated ground" (Il.18.98–104). Author's translation.

white poplar trees or tall pines hewn by craftsmen (Sarpedon 16:483–484), or as wheat and barley mown by farmers (Achaeans and Trojans 11:67–71) – similes that represent death in battle as natural and poetic. Old king Priam wistfully reflects on the theme when he contrasts his imminent and dreadful bodily rending by his own dogs to the most exquisite bodily rending of a young warrior in battle who dies at the peak of manhood (22.66–73). While these examples are not explicitly sacrificial, they do idealize battlefield death.

Nonetheless the *Iliad* does indeed configure death as sacrifice in a handful of poetic renderings. We see this in similes, as when, for instance, Hippodamas dies as a bull being sacrificed to Poseidon: "[Achilles] stabbed Hippodamas in the upper back with his spear. Then Hippodamas exhaled (*'aisthe*) his spirit (*thumos*) and belched (*'ērugen*), as a bull belches when he is dragged for the Helikonian lord by young men, and the Earthshaker is pleased with them" (20:402–406). More subtly, we see it in the ascription of panting and gasping verbs to men, typically Trojans or their allies, who die in language similar to the gasping lambs who die in the oath-sacrifice of the *Iliad* – they die "gasping and deprived of spirit, for the bronze had taken away their strength" (*'aispairontas thumoū deuomenous; apo gar menos heileto chalkos* 3:293–294). On a narrative level, this ascription of gasping and panting verbs is arguably because the Trojans en masse are implied to be suffering the fate of oath-violators, stemming from the oath-sacrifice in Book 3 (Kitts 2005). Examples include Asteropaios, who exhaled (*'asthmainonta*) his *thumos* (spirit) when Achilles killed him at the beginning of his fight with the river god (21.182); Thracians who gasped (*'aspairontas*) when Diomedes and Odysseus slaughtered them in the night (10.521); while dying, Adamas gasped (*'āspair'*) like an ox dying by human blows (13.571); Medon exhaled (*'aisthmainōn*) as he was struck in the temple and fell from the chariot (5.585); and Asios' charioteer did the very same thing

[con't]. Achilles does say eventually that he would win that good fame (νῦν δὲ κλέος ἐσθλὸν ἀροίμην [18:121]), but it is after a long self-incriminating lament and his anticipation of the costs of his imminent rage on the mothers and wives of Troy (18:122–125). On Achilles' emotional depth, see Zanker 1994:10–27 and Cairns 2003:11–50.

(13.396). These gasping and panting verbs in verses for dying on the battlefield give the audience an unflinching view of the victims' last breaths.[6] By reading metaphor with Ricoeur (1981), we can see a figurative transference implied between dying in oath-sacrifice and dying in battle. These examples show that the sacrificial figuration of battlefield death runs very deep in Western imagination. We will return to this sacrificial figuration of dying humans when we explore the curses accompanying oath-sacrifices of the ancient Near East.

For contemporary sensibilities, though, it is arguably the Christian martyrologies that set the Western bar for sacrifice, despite abundant antecedents in classical Greek tragedy,[7] Greek political oratory,[8] Judeo-Christian theology (Hengel 1977, 1981), and biblical narrative (n.b. Levenson 1993, 2013). The first generations of Christians may have disparaged the actual sacrificial practices of Jews and pagans (1 Cor. 10:18–22), but the trope of sacrifice resounded through martyrologies and hagiographies, representing Christian deaths in the Roman arena as courageous self-sacrifices in the model of Christ. Moss (2010), Nasrallah (2012), and others have explored the uneasy tension between the call to Christian sacrifice in the form of selfless devotion and communal sharing (e.g., Romans 10:1–13, 12:1–6) versus the call to *imitatio Christi* unto death,[9] but it is fair to say that vicarious suffering is a conspicuous theme in the occasional epistle[10] and in the martyr acts. Rather than view Christ's crucifixion as a one-time salvific event (as in, e.g., Matthew 20:28, Hebrews 7:27, 9:11–14, Philippians 2:5–9, Romans 5:6–11, 1 Corinthians 5:7), these texts, particularly the martyr acts of Tertullian, Cyprian, Origen of Alexandria, and Ignatius of Antioch, enjoin *imitatio* in the Roman arena as an opportunity to participate in suffering with Christ. Thus Ignatius proclaims: "Let there come upon me fire and cross and encounters with beasts, mutilation, tearing apart, scattering of bones,

---

[6] See too Christopher Faraone on my insights (2019:309).

[7] For example, *Seven against Thebes* 472–480; *Antigone* 1012–1017; *Iphigenia at Aulis* 1552–1558.

[8] Pericles' Funeral Oration (Thucydides 2.34–46) (Fordham University Ancient History Sourcebook).

[9] Cf. Mark 8:34–38. [10] For example, Gal. 2:20; Rom. 8:36; 2 Cor. 4:10–11.

mangling of limbs, grinding of the whole body, evil tortures of the devil, only that I may attain to Jesus Christ."[11] So too Origen: "Bring wild beasts, bring crosses, bring fire, bring tortures. I know that as soon as I die, I come forth from the body, I rest with Christ."[12]

That these deaths were conceived not only as *imitationes* but as martial deaths is evident in the Christian co-option of Roman language of the military *devotio* and *sacramentum*: "Oh, what was that spectacle of the Lord, how sublime, how great, how acceptable to the eyes of god through the solemn *sacramentum* and *devotio* of his army" (Cyprian Epistulae 10.2.3[13]; n.b. Barton 1994, 2002). For Christian audiences to the actual martyr deaths or to the hagiographies built on them, configuring deaths in the Roman arena as acts of witnessing (*martyrion*, properly speaking[14]), supported by a military oath of commitment (*sacramentum*[15]), extended the valorization of sacrificial death to heroic death, earning for the Christian sufferer a certain Roman *virtus*.[16] It is argued that during the Empire period disenfranchised gladiators came to be seen not as debased slaves but as defiant heroes taking pleasure in the struggle up to the moment of death (Barton 1994:20). Similarly, disenfranchised Christians, at least in their rhetoric, when subjected to torture in the arena inverted their stature, dying not as tepid, impotent victims but as consecrated warriors committed to dying the good death (Shaw 1996; Grig 2002). For Christian audiences, the Greco-Roman ideal of resolute heroic death is said to have combined with the pathos undergirding biblical expectations that the messiah was to suffer and die (alluding to, e.g., Isaiah 53), to create an ethos establishing Christians who endured humiliating deaths in the arena as victorious warriors who won glory in the life to come (Collins 1994; Cobb 2008; Moss 2010).

Of course, Christians were not the only people in world religions to embrace virtuous suffering. Shī'i commemorations famously engage with

[11] Romans 5.2. Translation by Cobb 2008:3.
[12] *Dialogue with Heraclides*. From Droge and Tabor 1992:149.
[13] Translation in Barton 1994. [14] See Kitts 2018b.
[15] Itself a combination of devotion, consecration, and execration (Barton 1994:52).
[16] Schultz points out that the Romans themselves are unlikely to have perceived the deaths of gladiators as sacrifices (2010:517, n1).

similar themes (Haider 2018), as do Sikh martyrdom tales (Fenech 2018) and Liberation Tigers of Tamil Eelam (LTTE) celebrations (Schonthal 2018). Apparently, the notion resonates across religious contexts.[17]

Literary Accounts of Premodern Human Ritual Killings

It is obvious from the foregoing discussion that the perception of humans as sacrificial victims had a special hold on ancient imaginations, at least as represented in texts. Watts reminds us that stories of human sacrifice and actual practices are two different things (2007). The stories typically explain ritual slaughters that no longer occur but continue to fascinate us – often ascribed to ancestors or foreigners – whereas archaeological evidence only rarely supports the practice, albeit with notorious exceptions.[18] In literature, though, methods of ritual killings are varied and graphic: they range from slitting throats, burnt offering, beheading, burying alive, drowning, halving, dismemberment, and exposing to the sun, and there are occasional reports of anthropophagy. Rationales for the practice are equally varied. Some scholars take pains to distinguish ritual killings from human sacrifices, claiming that sacrifices are by definition "sacrifices to," as to a god or hero, whereas a ritual killing tends to be a larger category that can occur outside of, for instance, a regular cycle of festivals (Schultz 2010). However, as we shall see, in literary reports involving human victims the line between sacrifice and ritual killing is artificial, since multiple meanings radiate from "sacrificial" events.

This polysemy is consistent with newer trends in ritual studies, which acknowledge a variety of dimensions to ritual communication – for example, poetic, iconic, somatic, metaphoric, even discursive. A host of artistic and imaginative dimensions transcend purely political or socially strategic purposes.[19] These various dimensions likely interpenetrate for participants

---

[17] See Kitts, ed. for overviews of the theme (2018c). N.b. the studies of very ancient funerary rituals that ponder apparently acquiescent deaths of otherwise healthy sacrificial victims – for example, Pollock in Laneri (2007:209–222) on Ur and on the death of households.

[18] N.b., McCarty (2019) on Punic Tophets and *mlk* rites.

[19] For summaries, see Kitts 2017, 2018a.

and witnesses and communicate syncretistically. We should acknowledge too a variety of ritual registers – from casual and celebratory to elevated and menacing – that surely bear on the ritual effects. While traditions all over the world could be invoked to show this polysemy, we will confine ourselves here to brief summaries of three somewhat sensational premodern traditions that can be shown to embed human sacrifice in complex cosmologies and etiologies. They are Aztec, Chinese, and Classical Greek.

Aztec Human Sacrifices

Aztec cosmology is built upon the Mesoamerican understanding of cyclical time. Based on the Florentine Codex compiled by Bernardino de Sahagún in the sixteenth century, Graziano points out that, by Aztec understanding, the world had been destroyed four previous times, followed by repopulation with new beings. At the time of the Spanish conquest, "the Aztecs believed that existence under the fifth sun had reached its zenith, that the stages of creation had exhausted all possibilities, and that the forthcoming destruction would be the final one ending the world and humanity forever" (1999:40).

To avert this cataclysmic end, various forms of debt payment were practiced, including human sacrifice. As the gods four different times had cast themselves into an enormous subterranean fire to restore the sun and moon and other celestial bodies – by an elaborate metamorphosis and journey beneath and then above the surface of the earth (Graziano 1999:41; Carrasco 2013:218) – so now earthly creatures were expected to be killed in ritual sacrifice and to undergo a similar metamorphosis. Losing their corporeal coverings through death, humans' divine essences went into the underworld to await resurrection in the form of new bodies, which again would be sacrificed. This need for continuous human sacrifice was due to the gods' weariness with their own cosmogonic self-sacrifices and to their need for nourishment with blood ("precious water"), which gods obtained through human sacrifice as well as war, gladiatorial combats, and other blood-spilling activities (Carrasco 1999:82). Humans were understood as privileged to play this role in nourishing the gods. The gods created them and were intimately connected to them, as manifested in the way sacrificed humans were transformed into god-images when they died

(Carrasco 2013:218). The blood of sacrificed humans was seen as cosmically restorative and ritual sacrifices as necessarily continuous.

Hence, wartime activities could be occasions for accruing captives to be killed not as simple "sacrifices to" but rather as players within this elaborate cosmological scheme, itself built on a rich pantheism. Auspicious points on sacred landscapes – sites of divine beings, temples, and venerable neighbor-hoods – were understood to absorb the blood of war victims sacrificed by Aztec kings and priests. The blood was deposited at double-helix-shaped portals where the divine world was seen to intersect with the human (Carrasco 1999:148, 2013:218).[20] Such sacrifices were performed with ele-vated ceremony. The rituals were sensorily titillating, blending costumes, dances, music, and smells – a virtual smorgasbord of experiences designed to reach participants at multiple points on the bodily sensorium.

The Aztec ceremony of Toxcatl illustrates some of this elaborate cosmovision as well as its titillating effects. Considered a debt payment to chief god Tezcatlipoca ("lord of the smoking mirror"), a captive of war – one without bodily blemish, suitably slender and trained in the arts of music, singing, speaking, walking, and flower arranging – after a year of prepara-tion consummated by twenty days of sexual pleasure with four wives, was killed on a ceremonial platform. His heart was then extracted and offered to the sun. He was beheaded, his skull was emptied and placed on a skull rack, and his body was tenderly lowered to the ground. This *teotl ixiptla*, divine image of Tezcatlipoca, was understood as not a symbolization of the god but as a transformed being: the young warrior became the god, was absorbed by the god, was possessed by the god. On his way to death he was adorned with all manner of divine attributes and was sighed over by the people he encountered. It was said that he understood his role, ascended to his place of death without resistance, and broke his flutes and whistles on the steps to his death. According to Sahagún, "And this betokened our life on earth. For he who rejoiced, who possessed riches, who sought, who esteemed our lord's sweetness, his fragrance – richness, prosperity – thus

---

[20] This notion of profuse saturation of the human world by the divine will linger through contact with the Christian worldview, resulting in a rich syncretism, as described by Graziano (1999:101–107).

ended in great misery. Indeed it was said 'No one on earth went exhausting happiness, riches, wealth'" (quoted in Carrasco 1999:121). If Sahagún is to be trusted, this last statement suggests that the Aztecs were not indifferent but fully aware of the enormous personal cost for one chosen to be *teotl ixiptla*.

Chinese Human Sacrifices

With its approximately seven millennia of settlement, China cannot be deemed a monolith in terms of religious practices, but we can explore a few illuminating reports of human sacrifice. Alongside a wealth of archaeological data dating back to the Neolithic Age (5000–2000 BCE) (Yates 2013), there are textual reports that can give us some perspective on how the practice was understood at different periods and places.

The oracle bone inscriptions of the late Shang (the fifteenth to eleventh centuries BCE) are perhaps the most sensational early reports and appear to combine sacrificial practices with war. They detail methods of human killing such as beheading, splitting the body into halves, dismembering, beating to death, chopping, bloodletting, burning, burying alive, drowning, and exposing to the sun (Wang Ping 2008). According to Shelach (1996:13), the Qiang, agricultural neighbors of the Shang,[21] were the objects of Shang ritual killings in more than half of the 14,197 cases, their decapitations were reported with a special vocabulary distinct from that for sacrificing animals, and they are the only ethnic group named on the oracle bones. The inscriptions report that the Qiang were hunted for the purpose of ritual sacrifice, making them likely war captives. As Yates explains, war was considered essential for providing the raw meat and blood of enemy soldiers for "the open-air altar of soil that was the symbol of the state," and for maintaining the continued goodwill of the spirits of dead ancestors. If the ancestors were not fed meat, grain, and liquor, they were believed to die and thus could not help their descendants. These notions about warfare and the nurturance of the state continued up to the end of the imperial period in the early twentieth century, and, according to Yates, "to the extent that the

---

[21] Contrary to some claims about the pastoral Qiang, pastoral nomadizing was not introduced to China until the first millennium BCE. See Shelach 1996.

Chinese saw the person of the ruler as a religious figure, the Son of Heaven, who was responsible for maintaining the harmony of the cosmos and for the continuation of the sacrifices to his ancestors and the preservation of the imperial line, to that extent warfare was also seen as a religious activity" (2013; see too ter Haar 2019).

Feeding the soil and spirits with human flesh and blood is rooted in more complex assumptions, however, as Jimmy Yu investigated in his work on Chinese self-sacrifice (2012). As he sees it, based on the homology between the body and the cosmos, the human body traditionally was understood as a cosmic instrument. Hence ritual activities that might be thought to injure the body, such as auto-cremation, bodily slicing, fasting, and blood writing, could be understood to boost natural relationships, not only in the earliest literary evidence but up into the seventeenth century. For instance, auto-cremation, or self-immolation, was not only a devotional practice of Buddhist bodhisattvas (as adulated in the Lotus Sutra [Benn 2007]) but a self-sacrificing practice of legendary shaman-kings who strove through self-immolation to induce the sky to rain (Yu 2012:115–139). Just as complexly, filial slicing – for example, slicing one's thigh – to offer one's flesh for consumption by ailing parents not only was rooted in the Confucian virtue of filial piety but must be also understood against a larger practice of anthropophagy. Aside from situations of famine and similar deprivations, ingesting the flesh of humans was (1) tied to folk medicine, where eating human flesh was thought to restore health and aid in acquisition of supernatural powers; (2) tied to the Buddhist practice of meritorious self-sacrifice wherein offering one's flesh might invite blessings from heavenly realms; and (3) tied to political maneuvers such as wars of conquest and rituals of revenge – as when despised Ming eunuch Liu Jin was consumed by his enemies to highlight his defeat (Yu 2012:64–73).

At the level of folk medicine, legends indicate that certain monarchs supposedly demanded children's flesh to prolong life, and in esoteric Tantrism eating the human heart was thought to enable the acquisition of power and immortality (Yu 2012:68–69). Infanticide occurred for other reasons, aside from extra mouths to feed in times of famine. The fourth-century Daoist millenarian sect called the Immortals, harkening back to the Yellow Turbans, reputedly drowned their children when military defeat was imminent, telling them, "We congratulate you on first ascending to the palace of the immortals! We shall follow you shortly." According to Wicky Tse, this gave the act of infanticide a religious meaning and, broadly speaking, religious thinking gave meaning to violent movements in imperial China (2020:293–294).

While to contemporary readers these reports may seem lurid, they are better appreciated against an understanding of the human body as a ritual instrument that could "influence heaven, bring rain, ward off ghosts, destroy artillery, counteract sorcery, and predict future events" (Yu 2012:136). Here too the sacrifice of humans is not simply "sacrificing to," but part of larger cosmological dreams and dynamics.

Greek Human Sacrifices

It is surely the mythology of Classical Greece that is most rife with human sacrifice, although the practice is condemned in nearly all the literature (Bonnechere 2013:¶3). Here too human sacrifice is sometimes combined with anthropophagy. Since Hesiod's *Works and Days*, the killing and eating of one's own was deemed something only animals (Works and Days 276–278) or, for Plato, mythic tyrants do (Rep. 8.565d–566). Yet legends abound for both aberrant behaviors. The legends are often punctuated by themes of revenge.

Eating one's enemies is figuratively sating, if not exactly pleasurable, in our oldest Greek epic (Hecuba viz Achilles' liver, *Iliad* 24.212–13; Hera viz the Trojans, Il.4:32–36; Achilles viz Hector Il.22.346–347), whereas in myth eating humans is deplored. When Tantalos cooked his son Pelops to be eaten in a stew for the gods, he brought upon himself and his descendants Demeter's curse for five generations[22] and apparently passed the custom onto his grandson Atreus, who served his brother Thyestes a stew with the flesh of two of Thyestes' sons.[23] The cycle famously ended when Atreus' son Agamemnon sacrificed his daughter Iphigenia to enable safe sailing to

---

[22] Griffiths, "Tantalus." *Oxford Classical Dictionary Online*. https://doi.org/10.1093/acrefore/9780199381135.013.6218

[23] March, "Atreus." *Oxford Classical Dictionary Online*. https://doi.org/10.1093/acrefore/9780199381135.013.941

the Trojan War, after which his wife murdered him and their son committed matricide with other sensational crimes along the way, as dramatized by Aeschylus and Euripides. Whereas the tragedians are very exercised by the immorality of such behaviors, there are other tales whose outcomes are more ambiguous, as when Procne killed and served up her son in a stew for Tereus after he raped her sister and cut out her tongue. The two sisters were transformed into a swallow and a nightingale and Tereus was transformed into a hoopoe.[24] The two themes, sacrifice and anthropophagy, combine in the Arcadian cult of Zeus Lykaios, where, according to a few accounts (Bremmer 2007), the innards of a sacrificed boy mixed with other flesh were eaten by a youth who thereafter was transformed into a wolf for a period of nine years, during which he was forbidden to eat human flesh if he were to return to his former shape. Alternatively, Lykaon ostensibly sacrificed a baby on the site and poured its blood on the altar, thereafter becoming a wolf, or, he offered it to Zeus, who in disgust hurled a bolt of lightning at the house of Lykaon and turned him into a wolf. The stories can be made to support various etiologies, but it is obvious that the line between sacrifice and anthropophagy is thin in these crimes. What human sacrifice and anthropophagy have in common, minimally, is that both are understood as religiously transgressive.

In Euripides, eight out of seventeen tragedies report human sacrifices (Henrichs 2000:177; Bonnechere 2013:¶6[25]), with heroic tristesse coloring especially the sacrifices of Iphigenia at Aulis and Trojan Polyxena (Bremmer 1983, 2007:64[26]). Although we never witness a sacrificial killing on stage, spoken reports exploit sacrificial rhetoric to highlight the perverted nature of such killings. For instance, the verb *sphazdein*, to slaughter, a powerful verb attributed to animal death since Homer, is said to connote

[24] Less ambiguous are the man-eating monsters of the *Odyssey* and the child-swallowing Kronos in the Theogony, who are seen to hark back to a darker age.

[25] In Bonnechere's opinion, Euripides, although relegating these sacrifices to a primordial past, nonetheless assumed they once occurred. Legends are abundant wherein human sacrifice is replaced with animal sacrifice (2013:¶32).

[26] See Van Straten for the famous vase painting showing Polyxena being slaughtered (1995:119[V422]).

more violence and bloodshed than *thyein*, a loftier verb referring to sacrifice more generically, as we see in *Hecuba* when Polyxena's sacrifice over the tomb of Achilles is described with cognates of the former (at 41, 109, 119, 135, 305), except when Odysseus diplomatically reports her death to the girl's mother (at 223) (Henrichs 2000:177–180; Bremmer 2007:60–61).[27]

But it is the Oresteia of Aeschylus, especially *Agamemnon*, that is most saturated with ritual and sacrificial vocabulary, however perverted for tragic effect. It starts with *proteleios* (Ag.65) in the parados, a word typically referring to preliminary animal sacrifices performed before marriage, but here perverted to indicate men slain in preliminary battles before the destruction of Troy (Zeitlin 1965:465). It continues with reference to the failure of libations and unfired sacrifices to assuage divine wrath (Ag.69–71; Zeitlin 1965:465), similar to the failure of sacrificed cattle to save Troy or Cassandra (Ag.1169–1171). Sacrificial rhetoric permeates Cassandra's visions of the crimes stemming from the bloody slaughter (*androsphageion*) of Thyestes' children (1090–1092) and of other crimes, including the killing of Iphigenia (238–240). Clytemnestra's actual slaying of Agamemnon is rendered as the three libations typical of a sacrificial feast, not of wine here, but of blood. Clytemnestra likens these to the three blows she gave him, after which he gasped out the *sphagēn* of his blood (1384–1390) (Zeitlin 1965:474). The Oresteia is steeped in sacrilegious themes, with perverted sacrifices, libations, and curses right up to Clytemnestra's reported blood libations over the tomb of Agamemnon (Zeitlin 1966:653) and to the struggle between Orestes and the Erinyes over blood bonds. It is as artistically sophisticated in disparaging the uses and misuses of religion as anything we might find today.

Last but not least, the human sacrifices on the funeral pyre of Patroclus in *Iliad* 23 are thought to be similarly disparaged (says Bonnechere 2013:¶2): hence the mind of Achilles – "evil were the deeds he contemplated in his mind" (23:176; 21:19[28]). Yet the urge for *poinē*, or revenge, in the war poem is not incomprehensible. Instead, the expression of this urge may be grasped in terms of what Fernandez has called a "ritual leitmotif," which effectively thickens and transforms the understanding of audiences by

[27] She is not deceived. [28] κακὰ δὲ φρεσὶ μήδετο ἔργα.

connecting a single scene to a primordial pattern or canonical ideal, often through the deployment of religious symbols and vocabulary that are especially volatile to interpretation.[29] Thus, despite some comparative realia for the sacrifices (on which see Hughes 1991; Kitts 2008), here we investigate the representation of the twelve Trojan boys captured and then killed on the pyre of Patroclus as peppered with ritual symbols and vocabulary that disseminate a ritual leitmotif for revenge killing.

First, the boys are killed, and are vowed to be killed, by the verb *deirotomeō* (23:174–176), or *appodeirotomeō* (18.336–337), referring to cutting the throat. Unlike *thyein* or *sphazdein*, these verbs built on *tamnō*, I cut, are concrete, literal, and unmistakable in their effects. We see this in the *Iliad*'s oath-sacrifices, where the simple *tamnō* is used for cutting the throats of the lambs/boar "with the pitiless bronze" (3:292[30]; 19:266), after which the lambs, deprived of strength, gasp out their lives (3:293–294; discussed earlier). Second, Achilles' confessed motive for the human sacrifices is *cholos* – I will cut their throats, *cholōtheis* for the death of Patroclus (18:337; again at 23:23). One of a handful of expressive anger words in the *Iliad*, *cholos* is characterized by a burning volatility (Kitts 2010) that distinguishes it from *kotos*, a smoldering anger lingering in hearts until it can be expressed, and from *mēnis*, an apocalyptic wrath associated with divinities and with Achilles at 1:1 and 21:523 (Frisk 1946; Cairns 2003; Walsh 2005). *Cholos* is indeed the most frequent word for anger (ninety-seven occurrences; Considine 1969) and even among the gods *cholos* is urgent: it is incurable, says Poseidon (15:217); Athene can barely restrain it (8:461); Hera cannot restrain it at all (8:460); it drives Poseidon (13:206), Hera (24:55), Apollo (1:9), even the river Xanthos (21:136) over the course of the war (Kitts 2010:13–19). *Cholos* is compared to the wild moil and toil stirred up by Zeus around the corpse of Patroclus when it is said that neither Ares

---

[29] Ritual leitmotivs, according to Fernandez, function similarly to metaphors by thickening and transforming experiences. They can "fill out this universe of religious experience giving it resonance, a thick complexity and potency, which the discussion of the paradigm of metaphors – however basic – does not fully capture" (Fernandez 1977:126). Discussed in Kitts 2008, 2010.

[30] καὶ ἀπὸ στομάχους ἀρνῶν τάμε νηλέϊ χαλκῷ (3.292).

nor Athene would have found fault with the slaughter even should *cholos* have overcome one of them (17:398–401). Third, *poinē* impresses ritual shape onto the expression of Achilles' *cholos* beginning as early as *Iliad* 21, when he captures those twelve Trojan youths, "stunned like fawns," to be sacrificed as *poinē* (21:27–29) on Patroclus' funeral pyre.[31] A family of related vocabulary built around *tinō*, I pay a price, has been argued to explain *poinē* as material exchange (Wilson 2002), but revenge killings associated with *poinē* in the *Iliad* are not always so precise. They range from explicit exchanges (e.g., Zeus' promise to Hector at 17:205–208), to nonspecific, wartime revenge (e.g., Akamas at 14:483–484; Patroclus at 16:398), to smoldering violence that can barely be constrained (on Achilles' new shield at 18:498–502), to marked killings such as this, wherein *poinē* is a poetic extension of *cholos* (Kitts 2010:25–26). By harnessing this rhetoric of *poinē*, the poetic tradition impresses ritual shape – a ritual leitmotif – on the killings of *Iliad* 23, which elevates them to a higher register – a ritual register – than simple battlefield carnage or commercial exchange.

Finally, the pre-cremation feast and the funeral itself impart an ominous mood to these killings.[32] The oxen sacrificed (*sphaʒdomenoi*) for the pre-cremation feast are cut down bellowing (23:30–33, as Autenrieth translates *orechtheon*[33] or possibly rattling[34]) – the only reference to sounds made by animals slaughtered for food – and their blood flowing around the corpse of Patroclus is so profuse that it could be caught in cups (23:34). Blood is never mentioned in the *Iliad*'s other commensal sacrifices. The next day many different animals are thrown onto the pyre to burn with Patroclus, including two dogs whose throats are cut (*deirotomēsas* again; 23:174) followed by the

---

[31] Kitts 2010; 2005:65–73.

[32] Mood itself is an item of aesthetic analysis (Morgan 2012:22–25, 33) applicable to rituals.

[33] Autenrieth 1958:232.

[34] Liddell and Scott 1968:1248. www.perseus.tufts.edu/hopper/morph?l=o%29re%2Fxqeon%26la=greek%26can=o%29re%2Fxqeon0%26prior=a)rgoi\%26d=Perseus:text:1999.01.0133:book=23:card=1%26i=1#lexicon. It is in any case a noisy death.

twelve Trojan captives, whom Achilles throws on the pyre, "destroying
them with the bronze." Considering this vivid vocabulary of killing and
blood, it seems indisputable that these human sacrifices are rendered as
more than simple "offerings to" and are embedded instead in a semantic
field conveying emotional extremes and the ritualized expression of ven-
geance. From all these examples, we can see that human sacrifice is rarely
a narrow "offering to" but instead is mired in complex cosmological
understandings and ritual dynamics.

2 Theories of Sacrifice

Embryonic Theories

Although we typically understand sacrificial theory as beginning in the nineteenth century, it should be noted that millennia-old thinking offers what
might be called embryonic theories. Evaluating these is complex because the
Bible and the Vedas, for instance, do not offer explicit ideologies or necessarily
reflect static ritual conventions. Indeed, for the sacrificial procedures in
Leviticus, it is argued that the biblical writers were not interested in reprodu-
cing convention, but instead in masking changes to it, which would explain the
motivation for writing about sacrifice in the first place (Watts 2006:127–130).
For the Vedas, priestly discussions of sacrifice were also ostensibly prescrip-
tive, aiming for a ritual ideal, but scholars observe variances among texts
(McClymond 2008:35), and an increasing discomfort with bloody offerings
over time (Parpola 2007). Classical Greek perspectives were notoriously
controversial. Whereas Hesiod and the Homeric poems render animal sacrifice
as the mark of the current age, Empedocles was repulsed by the practice,
equating it with devouring kin. The Orphics and Pythagoreans are claimed to
have been similarly repulsed. Although we cannot cover all ancient speculation
here, we can summarize some well-known embryonic theories that problematized the practice of sacrifice.

Biblical and Christian Sacrifice

In the biblical case, of the five major types of sacrificial offering in Leviticus
1–7 – burnt offering (*'ōlāh*), grain offering (*minhah*), sacrifice of well-being

(*ʒebah shalamim*), sin/purification offering (*hatta't*), and guilt offering
(*'asham*) (Gilders n.d.) – the *'ōlāh*/burnt offering takes pride of place. It
is first in nearly all lists and because it is not a meal shared with the people
and God but rather destroyed in fire, it might be considered taxing to the
community's resources (Watts 2006). The priority of a completely burned
offering has been explained variously, but Watts argues that the *'ōlāh* is seen
as a pure gift, the purest form of divine service by the temple priests. This is
supported by narratives of the sacrifice of children – Abraham and Isaac,
Jephthah and his daughter, Mesha of Moab and his son – which all describe
child sacrifice as an *'ōlāh*, a burnt offering, implying the ideal of selfless
devotion to God on the part of parents (despite fearful contexts and the
explicit prohibition of child sacrifice in other texts[35]). Watts endeavors to
show how the priority of burnt offerings is of a piece with second millennium BCE Ugaritic and Hittite ritual practices and how in the first millennium the practice of burning victims, whether completely or partially,
spread from northwest Syria to Mesopotamia and elsewhere among
Israel's neighbors. It continued to influence Jewish and Christian imaginations after the fall of the Jewish temple, which effectively eliminated animal
sacrifices in biblical tradition. According to him, in the early centuries
thereafter total devotion to God came to be gauged by risking death,
construed as a sacrifice, due to religious persecution.

However, other scholars stress different sacrifices and offer interpretations unique to those. For Janzen, the *hatta't* and guilt offerings as responses
to public, inadvertent sins function as pledges that the sinner will not act
against God's moral order in the future (2020:11). Instead of being pure
gifts, these sacrifices initiate social commitments for people understood to
have strayed from sovereign law at potentially lethal cost. Eberhart's
summary of the different vocabulary for sacrifice concludes that each
term has an individual profile but the comprehensive term *qorban*, indicating
to draw near, to bring near, "captures the dynamic movement of sacrificial
material toward the sanctuary and ultimately toward God who, according to
the priestly concepts, resides there" and enjoys the "pleasing odor" of
sacrifice (2011:23). Klawans (2001) explores sacrificial acts as combining

---

[35] Levenson (1993) remains most eloquent on this theme.

two notions, for which human and divine acts can be understood as some-what analogous. First there is an emphasis on a state of ritual purity (*imitatio dei*): ritually pure priests, like God, exercise complete control over the life and death of living beings – including selecting, killing, and looking inside victims. Relatedly, just as God appears on earth as a consuming fire, sacrificer-priests destroy parts of the victims in flames. Second, and simi-larly to Eberhart, Klawans notes that just as God enjoins the people to build a sanctuary where he/she might dwell among them (Exod. 25:8), priests are concerned with attracting divine presence through animal sacrifices – "the pleasing odor to God" – which leads us back to the notion of purity, as God will not abide in a land defiled by idolatry, sexual transgression, and murder. These are all just shreds of complex theories that build upon earlier theories (e.g., Milgrom 1998, in Watts 2007), but enough to show that, although the biblical authors (particularly P) did not articulate a concise theory of sacrifice, a clear dynamism is ascribed to sacrifice in all cases. These are not empty rituals but deliberate efforts to connect with and sway divine power.

Although Christians came to reject Jewish as well as Greco-Roman practices of animal sacrifice, biblical rhetoric about sacrifice clearly reso-nated with early Christians. As Daly sees it, the Christian co-option of Jewish sacrificial notions in the early centuries CE was based on a "heightened awareness of the abject frailty and sinfulness of human life over against the transcendent holiness and otherness of God" (2003 [1990]:346). Atonement thus became a dominant theme in Jewish sacrifices overall and shaped symbolic understandings of Christ's death as an atoning blood sacrifice, for "[w]ithout the shedding of blood there would be no forgiveness of sins" (Hebrews 9:22). Daly distinguishes atonement from expiation and propitiation (2009:35–36), but it is fair to say that all of these presume a divine-human estrangement in need of remedy. Of the various conceptions of Christ's sacrifice as this remedy, for Daly it is the servant theme (e.g., Isaiah 53:10–12) that most resonates, wherein Christ gives his life as a ransom for many (Mark 10:45; Matthew 20:28) (2009:53) and in obedient self-offering to the Father for the salvation of humanity (2003 [1990]:349–350). With two thousand years of further interpretation, the Christian picture is hardly simple, but one of Daly's central points is the gradual dematerialization and increasing spiritualization of Christian sacrifice, built on a number of biblical paradigms understood to represent selfless giving, from the Akedah through 4 Maccabees (2009:29, 40, 48). In antiquity this shift was boosted by at least four social changes: the end of actual Jewish templar sacrifices in 70 CE; the metaphorization of Christian martyrdom as sacrifice; the end of public sacrifices as religious foci; and the rise in reading, singing, translating, and commenting on scriptural passages as primary religious acts. These all contributed to the internalization of Christian religiosity and the end of sacrificial practices by the fourth century (Stromsa 2015).

Vedic Sacrifice

Sacrifice appears to have been problematized very early in Vedic ritual texts. Over centuries of textual development (the Śrauta Sūtras are dated 800–200 BCE), reports of Vedic animal sacrifice hint at ambivalence about the killing act. Ambivalence is implied in the fastidious ritual control mandated of the sacrificer, explicit statements and gestures identifying him with his victim, the development of quiet suffocation as a means for slaying the animal, and the removal of the killing act from the sacred enclosure; similarly removed is preparing and taking the food of sacrifice (Heesterman 1984:122–123; 1993:33). A high tension between these ordered elements of ritual sacrifice and the threat of catastrophic annihilation should the elements get out of hand (Heesterman 1993:26–29), is said to be palpable in some early texts, among them the Mahabharata, a war story surrounded by ritual sacrifices at beginning and end. For Heesterman, although the tangible purpose of sacrifice is generally a festive meal, the domestication of sacrificial killing in Vedic ritual belies the fact that sacrifice once "was itself the apogee of the warrior's violent way of life" and "[o]ver the whole of the orderly and obsessively regulated vedic ritual there still hangs the dark cloud of a heroically violent world where gods and asuras are for ever fighting each other in endlessly recurring rounds of conflict" (Heesterman 1984:125). In his view an original violence to sacrifice thus was felt and managed by ritual control.

The tension between ritual control and destruction is echoed in legendary cosmogonic events, such as the primordial sacrifice of Purusa, where the primal man is dismembered to break down the unitary and stable universe into multiplicity. Hence once Purusa was immolated his essence entered the horse, which was then immolated, and his essence entered the ox, which was then immolated, and his essence entered the goat, the essence of which entered the earth and plant life (Heesterman 1993:28; McClymond 2008:49). In the Purusa myth his sacrifice initiates an increasingly divisive (dis)order, which the ritual of sacrifice attempts to control. Sacrifice "dramatizes the tangled relationships to excess in order to disentangle them and separate the identities," says Heesterman (1993:33). If the ritual control implies discomfort, it is notable that Parpola too sees a pattern of diminishing violence in the Śunahśepa legend and the Aitareya Brāhmaṇa, which are argued to betray a vestige of human sacrifice as a practice that eventually became unpalatable (2007).

However, other scholars argue that the highlight on killing in these analyses is overly dramatic, is Judeo-Christian in bias, and skews the polythetic nature of Vedic sacrifice (McClymond 2008). The emphasis on killing, they contend, ignores the wide variety of materials oblated, not only animals, but grains, wine, milk, and ghee, and the rules and meta-rules for managing the oblations. Killing is not absent from the nonanimal sacrifices – soma stalks are "pounded to death"[36] – but the killing is combined with other ritual manipulations including chanting, skinning, slaughtering, handling of the carcass, and cooking and consuming it, which together form a complex whole. McClymond urges us to imagine such sacrifices as "organic complexes of activity rather than as a linear sequence of discrete procedures" (2008:54) and notes that victim killing is not particularly equated with violence (52).

Another contentious issue is blood. Whereas the precise placing of blood on the altar and the congregation is mandated in some biblical rituals (for "the life of the flesh is in the blood" [Lev. 17.11]) and

---

[36] One text urges soma sacrificers to think of someone they hate as they strike the soma stalks. On the other hand, McClymond observes that the plants do not die violently (bloodily?), which is why sacrificial scholars tend to ignore their deaths. Of course, nor do animals die violently, since they typically are suffocated (McClymond 2002:224–226).

bloodshed is stressed in popular theories (e.g., Girard, Burkert), in the Vedic offerings there is no blood spilling until after the animal is dead. The animal's death is not represented as a savage act but as a "quieting" by suffocation or strangling, ideally with no sound of protest at all. Instead of the biblical notion that "blood is the life," it is the victim's breath that is the life; breath is emphasized and managed. From these varying interpretations we can see that Vedic sacrifice too may have been controversial early on.

Classical Greek

Reconstructing the Classical Greek understanding of animal sacrifice is similarly complicated by its millennia-long tradition (from at least Hesiod to Porphyry), but three strands of sacrificial myth already were problematized in antiquity. These are associated with the Prometheus myth of Hesiod, Porphyry's etiology of the Athenian Bouphonia, and legends concerning Empedocles, the Pythagoreans, and Orphics. Brief summaries follow.

Hesiod's Prometheus myth establishes the foundation of Greek animal sacrifice in a rupture between gods and men initiated by the trickery of Titan Prometheus, an early friend to humankind. Famously at Mecone, where gods and men once dined together, he relegated the best portion of meat for humans and hid bones in fat for the divine portion. As a consequence Zeus hid fire from humans, whereupon Prometheus stole it for us. In punishment, Prometheus was bound to cliffs in Scythia where eagles continuously devoured his liver, whereas humans were punished by the gift of women, "beautiful evils" (Hesiod, Th.585) and "a great plague, [who] make their abodes with mortal men, being ill-suited to Poverty's curse but suited to Plenty ... as an evil for men and conspirers in troublesome works" (Hesiod, Th.545–613). Bound to women, men now scratch the stubborn earth for grain, partake only obliquely of immortality through their offspring, and communicate with the gods by killing and sacrificing animals: on earth humans enjoy cooked flesh, while the gods on Olympos enjoy the savory smoke of roasting bones and fat (Vernant 1989:21–86). Sacrificial rituals thus commemorate a severance between gods and men (by implication initially only males, according to Vernant[37]), which commensal rituals attempt to mitigate by establishing vertical as well as horizontal communication among divine and human participants in a sacrificial meal.

Porphyry's etiology of the Athenian Bouphonia (at the Dipolieia) supplements this theme with another primordial error. He recounts the "murder" (*phonē*) of an innocent plowing ox (*bous*) caught munching cakes and cereal offerings for Zeus Polieus. An angry farmer, by chance a resident alien, struck the ox dead with an ax. In remorse he buried the ox and fled in self-imposed exile. His blood guilt brought on famine. In response to the Delphic oracle citizens resurrected the ox by effigy and invited the farmer to return and kill it again, this time with their help, thereby ritually replacing the act of murder with an act of mock sacrifice. Then the ax was put on trial and exiled for murder, while the farmer was invited to shed the burdens of individual guilt by joining the polis, which eats sacrificed meat. He agreed provided that the community as a whole took part. The resulting ritual became known as the Bouphonia, literally ox-murder (*phonē*), supporting the double entendre between killing in sacrifice and killing in murder. The crimes here are multiple – the ox's, the farmer's, and the community's – which makes for a strange ritual etiology. Burkert famously saw in the effigy and trial a comedy of innocence, betraying an uneasiness with the whole process, although other theories have been proffered too (see summary in Katz 1992). It is in any case an elaborate justification for killing and eating a working ox, understood as a friend to humankind.

The initial remorse of the alien farmer who killed the ox signals a third strand of legends that reject animal sacrifice as murder. The most explicit rejection is by Empedocles, whose fifth-century BCE theory of metempsychosis denied that animals were lesser beings appropriate for sacrifice. Animal souls and human souls were not only equal but also interchangeable. After death animal souls transmigrated into humans and vice versa. To sacrifice an animal therefore was to risk committing murder, even of one's deceased relatives: "After his son has changed shape, his utter fool of a father slaughters him yet prays ... Deaf to any protests, the father

---

[37] Although *anthropoi*, the generic term for humankind, is used at Th.563 and 570.

makes an evil meal of him after slaughtering him . . . In the same way, a son can kill his father and children can kill their mother."[38] To avoid this sort of filicide, said Empedocles, Greeks ought to foreswear animal sacrifice. Although the oral traditions about him are ambiguous, Pythagoras also is said to have avoided sacrifices and eating meat. He is said to have embraced the theory of the transmigration of souls, as did the Orphics, although evidence for them is equally ambiguous.[39] According to Detienne, this refusal to participate in commensal sacrifices was based on a refusal to endorse the notion that gods could be sought through ritual bloodshed and a refusal to accept the rupture between gods and men stemming from Hesiod's story of the fall. In reaction, some Pythagoreans are said to have offered Apollo Genetor only nuts, spices, and grains that the earth spontaneously provides, these understood to be the shared repast humans enjoyed with the gods before animal sacrifice entered the world (Detienne 1994:44–47).

It seems significant that all of these Greek stories understand animal sacrifice as a regretful mark of the fallen human condition. It could be argued, though, that the Bouphonia may hide a tongue-in-cheek relish for ox meat. It is also notable that, however regrettable in theory, visual representations of seemingly happy processions to animal sacrifices are frequent on vases from the Archaic and Classical periods, suggesting at least that the ritual was a staple of religious life. Nonetheless representations of actual killing over altars are sparse, although Van Straten does show a few (1995:109 [R225], 110 [V147], 112 [V144]). There is also a vase showing the striking of an ox's head with a double-sided ax (115 [V148]) and, curiously, a Homeric and possibly unrealistic depiction in Van Straten's 115 [V141], which shows seven men holding up a full-grown ox, with three officials seemingly directing and one apparently cutting its throat, although there is no altar. There is a question of verisimilitude here, reported and disputed by Van Straten (1995:109–113).

---

[38] Emped. fr. B 137 D-K. T, quoted in Naiden (2020:484).

[39] On both see Huffman (2018).
   https://plato.stanford.edu/entries/pythagoras

Although these summaries of biblical, Judeo-Christian, Vedic, and Classical Greek illustrations are not comprehensive, they are enough to show that commentary about sacrifice is very old and that in ancient times the practice of sacrificing and eating animals was already seen as in need of explanation and ritual control (pace J. Z. Smith 2004, discussed in what follows).

Modern Theories

Modern commentary on religious sacrifice emerged in Western intellectual thought in the nineteenth century, when the rise of the modern disciplines of the social sciences coincided with the discovery of thriving cultures in non-Western parts of the world. Such discoveries provided fuel for speculation on the evolutionary development of culture, an idea that drew on Charles Darwin's theory of biological evolution. Anthropological fieldwork today provides no support for a single evolutionary stream of religious history; there is no singular progression from savagery to barbarism to civilization, as some social evolutionists would have it. Nonetheless these early theories of cultural evolution did lead to a series of important questions about sacrifice, such as why it is so common and whether there is a universal motivation for the practice.

Tylor (1832–1917)

One of the earliest modern theorists was Edward Burnett Tylor who, despite his nineteenth-century suppositions about "savages" and cultural evolution, understood early religion as primarily reasonable and based in natural observation (Evans-Pritchard 1965:26). In *Primitive Religion* Tylor opined that religion was born in early human observations about death, dreams, and altered states of consciousness, leading to the notion of animism, that the world is alive with spirits.[40] Reflecting on "phantoms"

---

[40] "At the lowest levels of culture of which we have clear knowledge, the notion of a ghost-soul animating man while in the body, and appearing in dream and vision out of the body is found deeply ingrained (not a vestige of something or a relic from which savage tribes have degenerated)" (1958:499).

(dreams,[41] shades of the dead, visions, etc.) understood to exist outside of the human body (1958:12), early humans came to embrace "souls" emanating from nonhuman as well as human beings, culminating in belief in guardian and nature spirits, and eventually in vastly superior beings such as gods. This led to his simple idea of religion as belief in spiritual beings. These beings were incorporeal, extraneous from us, and potentially in control of human destiny.

Tylor's earliest treatment of sacrifice was of funeral sacrifices, seen as gifts to the dead. Presuming the dead is animate, gifts to the dead were seen as a way of providing departed souls with food or weapons or clothes, "for whatever happens to the man may be taken to happen to the objects that lie beside him and share his fate, while the precise way in which the transmission takes place may be left undecided" (1958:69). In some cases the scale of funeral sacrifice rose to human sacrifice: "Men do not stop short at the persuasion that death releases the soul to a free and active existence, but they quite logically proceed to assist nature by slaying men to liberate their souls for ghostly uses (458). Tylor's clear assumption was that the dead soul was felt to live on and to be able to make use of sacrificial gifts, however costly.

In Tylor's view sacrificial practice expanded from the funerary context, to foundation sacrifices, to attempts at healing, to other distinctively religious experiences such as to "propitiate the earth spirits with a victim or to convert the soul of the victim himself into a protecting demon" (1958:106). The use of sacrifice was thus promiscuous, fitting many conceivable etiologies. It evolved from gift-giving to formal ceremonies such as substitution offerings wherein a part was offered in place of the whole, implying understanding of the substitution by the ritual's recipient. In the end sacrifice went from the actual gift, to animate beings existing outside the body, to ceremonial homage expressed by

---

[41] Spencer just after him (1882) saw the beginnings of religion in dreams, which "gave man the idea of his duality, and he identified the dream-self which wanders at night with a shadow-self which appears by day" (Evans-Pritchard 1965:23). See Spencer, *Principles of Sociology*, exerpted in Carter 2003:41–52.

a gift,[42] to self-abnegation seen as in itself virtuous: "that the virtue lies
in the worshipper depriving himself of something prized" (461–462).
Tylor supported this progression of sacrifice as a gift to a god ("as if he
were a man," 468) to a spiritual state of self-abnegation by a glance at
biblical sacrifices, where "sacrifice appears not with the lower conception
of a gift acceptable and even beneficial to a deity, but with the higher
significance of devout homage or expiation for sin" (excerpted in Carter
2003:20).

By today's standards Tylor's understanding of religion and sacrifice may
seem overly minimalist and tainted by his evolutionary assumptions about
lower savagery versus civilized religion. However, he wasn't entirely
disparaging about the early stages of religion, arguing, for instance, that
"[f]ully to understand an old world myth needs not evidence and argument
alone, but deep poetic feeling" (1958:35).

Frazer (1852–1941)

James G. Frazer too addressed diverse ethnographies from all over the
world, collecting reports of travelers into his twelve-volume work *The
Golden Bough*. His assumptions also reflected the evolutionary bias of the
times in that he proclaimed that religion began with magic, evolved to
religion, and finally evolved to science. For him, though, the earliest
religious impulse was rational: people strove to understand their world by
thinking and acting according to universal principles, particularly by the
principles of homeopathic (imitative) and contagious magic, which he saw
as the foundation of early religion.

His relevant accounts of sacrifice dealt with totemism, scapegoating,
and myths of dying and rising gods that he linked to regicide. Frazer
explained the sacrifice of totems in evolutionary terms, claiming that
"savages" identified more closely with animals than did Frazer's contemporaries (1951:616). Hence their deference for certain animals, such
as the bear for the Ainu. Although the Ainu kill and eat the bear and use

---

[42] "The offerings of meals and feasts to the dead may be traced at their last stage
into mere traditional ceremonies, at most tokens of affectionate remembrance of
the dead, or works of charity to the living" (1958:42).

its skin for clothing, they recognize the bear as an intelligent and powerful animal, and so atone for their killing by rearing bears with great kindness and killing them only with sorrow. He reported many examples of such "sacramental killings" of animals attributed godlike qualities, the deaths of which stir remorse for people who identify with them.

Frazer explained scapegoating in terms of the expulsion of evils. Although the scapegoat could be anything from a tortured goat to a divine cow (1951:655–661), its purpose ultimately was to rid the community of evils by absorbing them and then being driven out of the community. Not surprisingly, there is ambivalence when the scapegoat is a dying god, when the expulsion might invite sorrow as well as joy. Frazer noted a number of accounts of scapegoating in Western antiquity that occur in a context of feasting, reveling, and moral license, which invites us to ponder how many more purposes than expulsion of evils such festivals might promote.

Frazer's most famous legacy was his treatment of myths and rituals relating to dying and rising gods, whose deaths and rebirths were thought to herald the death and rebirth of grain. Frazer collected such myths from all over the world, although he interpreted them in terms of classical Western paradigms (1951:389–396). According to Frazer, these deaths were ritually accomplished by imitative magic, such as men violently destroying corn by cutting it and stamping it into pieces on the threshing floor and then grinding it. As a mythic example, he pointed out how in the season of death women ostensibly wept for dying Tammuz (e.g., Ezekiel 8:12–16) and then reputedly rejoiced when he was reborn in the spring. He related regicide to killing the god. At a certain stage in religious evolution, the king, who was accorded status and magical power, was thought to communicate with the god, to absorb the divine power, even to be godlike, until he was not. If the king were to weaken or die, everything around him, via both the contagion and imitative models of magic, might weaken or die too. Hence harvests, weather, peace, and political stability rested on his well-being. With sensational report after report, Frazer tried to show that the regicide of kings or their substitutes was ultimately aimed at rejuvenating the natural world and the rapport with the divine in response to a felt disorder

(1951:319–336, n.b. 326–327, 344–345). His application of this model was quite fluid, however. He noted that regicides may occur in response to situational factors or purely in response to a cycle of years, or be represented as a yearly process, as we see mimicked in countless myths of the violent death and rebirth of a vegetation god.

Although they certainly have taken root in popular thinking, Frazer's theories have been debunked by anthropologists and historians of religion, who criticize the theory for its imposition of classical Western paradigms and its glossing over of stark differences among societies. See Mark Smith on dying gods (2001/2003) and Jonathan Z. Smith on regicide (1973, 1990:81–93). Contrast, however, de Heusch (1985) on both notions.

Robertson Smith (1846–1894)

William Robertson Smith too was steeped in evolutionary assumptions, but his interest was less in the primitive theology of early peoples than in their institutions and shared rituals. Relative to Tylor and Frazer, Robertson Smith deemphasized belief in favor of received social obligations: "A man did not choose his religion or frame it for himself; it came to him as part of the general scheme of social obligations and ordinances laid upon him, as a matter of course, by his position in the family and in the nation" (1957:28, n.b. 16–20). It was only times of chaos, when the institutions seemed to fail, that nascent philosophizing about religion was born. His example was biblical sacrifice, which, he said, preceded its rationale and initially was its own end. Ideations of atonement, substitution, purification, redemption, and the like were invented to explain the sacrifice once the ritual tradition was broken, when the break with tradition gave rise to people's creative reflections about the reasons for the ritual in the first place. Until that occurs, the urge to perform traditions will overshadow belief in their efficacy.

His theses relevant to sacrifice may be broken into three, which overlap: kinship, commensality with a god – fostered through animal sacrifice – and totemism. In *The Religion of the Semites*, Robertson Smith emphasized that early religion was founded on kinship among humans by a bond of blood (or sometimes sealed by oath) and with a deity understood to be of the same blood stock (1957:50–51).[43] This bond was established by an act of communion "in which the god and his worshippers unite by partaking together of the flesh and blood of a sacred victim" (227, n.b. 275). Using the biblical evidence as exemplary, he noted that, unlike cereal offerings, animal sacrifice had a profound significance not as a mere payment of tribute, "but an act of social fellowship between the deity and his worshippers" (224), from which those outside the kinship group were typically excluded (275). Commensality was binding: the sacrament of a common meal was used to seal engagements and "[i]n every case the engagement is absolute and inviolable," constituting "a perfect obligation" (272).

On totemism, as no sharp demarcation was felt between the people and their god ("same blood stock"), and as gods and men were not felt to be entirely disengaged from animals (1957:85), there was a potential for kinship between gods and certain kinds of animal, just as there was kinship between humans and their gods. This three-way kinship was deeply felt:

> Now if kinship between the gods and their worshippers, on the one hand, and kinship between the gods and certain kind of animals, on the other, are deep-seated principles of Semitic religion, . . . we must necessarily conclude that kinship between families of men and animal kinds was an idea equally deep-seated, and we shall expect to find that sacred animals, wherever they occur, will be treated with the regard which men pay to their kinsfolk. (289)

This is evident because not all animals are sacrificed and eaten with the same ceremony. Totem, or sacred, animals are too much akin to the gods to be sacrificed and eaten casually, and when there is occasion for a totem feast, the animal is sacrificed with solemn ritual, essentially as a mystical sacrament (295). Citing many examples, Robertson Smith detects in this a lingering pious scruple about killing and eating flesh (303), but also a therianthropic appreciation for the animal as godlike and as kin. Hence it

---

[43] And often manifesting effusive presence at special places (1957:142) where one might seek sanctuary (148).

comes to pass that the totem animal may be bewailed as a sacrosanct victim representing not only the god but also the sacrificers themselves (431). The solemn mystery of its death is justified because only in killing and eating the totem animal can humans experience "communion with the godhead, by participation in holy flesh which is ordinarily forbidden to man" (312).

By emphasizing the bonds created in sacrificial rituals, Robertson Smith broke with his contemporaries. Sacrifice was not a gift made over to the gods, but an act of communion that reinforced the sacred bond of kinship among people, their god, and a sacrosanct victim (226–227). These ideas reverberated into the thinking of Freud and Durkheim, among others. However, as Hubert and Mauss point out, his theory cannot explain those sacrifices wherein the animal is entirely destroyed.

Freud (1856–1939)

Sigmund Freud was an intellectual maverick, offering over the course of his lifetime a rich slate of theories on not only psychological maturation but also on the nature of society, law, and religion. Especially in his early works, he too accepted the evolutionary theories of his day, indeed embellishing the theories of his predecessors in his search for the origins of exogamy, totemism, and ambivalence regarding the dead. It is in an early work, *Totem and Taboo* (1918) that we find an explicit account of sacrifice and violence in his description of the Oedipal complex.

As is well known, Freud based his Oedipal hypothesis on the principal figure in the Sophoclean tragedy of *Oedipus Tyrannos* (in Latin, *Rex*). The child of the Theban rulers Laius and Jocasta, Oedipus was prophesied to grow up to murder his father and marry his mother. To avoid such crimes, the parents had a shepherd take the child outside the city to be exposed, but in fact the child was given to a childless couple in Corinth. Growing up a passionate young man, Oedipus heard from the Delphic oracle that he would murder his father and marry his mother, so he fled from the Corinthian parents he thought were his biological sires. On a narrow road from Delphi, Oedipus met Laius, another passionate man, and killed him in an argument over the right of way. Arriving in Thebes, Oedipus found a kingless city suffering from a plague caused by the Sphinx, saved the city by solving the Sphinx's riddle, was welcomed into the city as a hero, and married its reigning widow, his mother, Jocasta. When due to another plague the seer Tiresias revealed the incestuous truth about Oedipus and Jocasta, Jocasta hung herself and Oedipus blinded himself with her brooch. Oedipus wandered blind to Colonus, accompanied by daughters Antigone and Ismene, and disappeared mysteriously (in *Oedipus at Colonus* 1645–1665). Of the four children born of this incestuous marriage, the two boys killed each other in a war over control of Thebes and the sisters Antigone and Ismene quarreled over burial rites for one of the brothers. In Sophocles' *Antigone* Antigone eventually hanged herself.

Freud saw in this tragic myth some underlying psychological dispositions residing in the human unconscious – a buried reservoir of feelings and psychological urges that he is credited with discovering. One disposition that correlates with his other works on religion (e.g., *Future of an Illusion* 1961 [1927]:42) is respect for the father-totem, whom he saw as lingering in the male unconscious as a father figure who once dominated his adolescent boys in an actual primal horde. The powerful father controlled the boys' sexual expression, which, due to their frustrated desire for sexual intimacy with the mother, led the boys to rise up and slay the father and to eat his flesh, thereby absorbing his power into themselves. This was followed by their remorse and eventual commemoration of the father-slaying in a totem feast, wherein a typically protected totem-animal, which it was taboo to kill, on occasion was ceremoniously slain in the father's place as well as eaten and lamented. At the same time, its killing was celebrated as a triumph – hence the ambivalence of the boys regarding the overcoming of the father. Another prohibition deriving from this primal crime was an incest taboo. Due to the boys' ambivalent feelings about the father and fear of a continued cycle of patricide, the coveted mother was now removed from the boys and revered in her own purity as untouchable. The primal crime of patricide thus resulted in two taboos – one against patricide and one against incestuous sex with the mother. These two taboos can be seen to echo the criminal consequences of Oedipus' murder of his father and sexual union with his mother in the tragedy of Sophocles.

Freud traces the myth further into both primal history and our unconscious cravings. Drawing on Robertson Smith, Freud read the totem feast as celebrating not only solidarity with the totem and the band of brothers but also the elevation of the father-totem to a father-god: "*the sacrificing community, its god, and the sacrificial animal were of the same blood* and members of the same clan" (italics in text 1946[1918]:176). The elevation of the totem-father to a god was spurred by the eventual domestication of totem animals and our estrangement from them (177, 190). As the animal-totem lost its power in our imaginations, the father-god came to transcend the totem, to be seen as all powerful and as demanding of a retributory sacrifice. One of the brothers volunteered to die as this retributory sacrifice, thereby cleansing the others of their primal crime.

Living in Catholic Austria at the time, Freud saw these core ideas in the Christian mythos. The patricide continues to resonate with us unconsciously as the original sin – that is, as the murder of the primal father and the wish to enjoy his divine status and the fruits thereof. Freud saw this as every boy's desire; men long to destroy authorities and make gods of themselves, but religion checks this urge by imposing a supernatural father figure onto human awareness along with the patricidal taboo. The primal guilt for this original murder is assuaged theologically by the voluntary death of Christ, by implication the brother who volunteered to die to absolve us of this primal crime. His mother is celebrated as a perennial virgin, chaste and untouchable. The patricidal crime is also assuaged ritually. Through the ceremony of the eucharist, Christ is now elevated into a savior figure, a god whose flesh and blood we continue to consume in unconscious commemoration of our primal crime.

Freud's Oedipal hypothesis, however creative, is often disputed as an unconscious driver of male psychological maturation. Nonetheless an enduring implication of Freud's thinking is that religious rituals may express and defuse destructive psychological urges, a notion replicated by René Girard.

Durkheim (1858–1917)

Emile Durkheim's approach to sacrifice was more sociological than his predecessors'. Indeed, he is credited with founding the discipline of sociology, as well as its first journal, *L'Année Sociologique*. Nonetheless the influence of the anthropologists Robertson Smith and Tylor is evident in his *Elementary Forms of Religious Life*, which was the culmination of decades of study into Australian totemic societies. Durkheim saw totemic societies as based in the same real human need and social experience as non-totemic societies, but also less contaminated by extraneous religious institutions and ideas and therefore a more pristine subject of study (2001:4–21).

Durkheim is perhaps best known for his division of the human experience into two categories – sacred and profane – a division he saw as the hallmark of religious thought (2001:36). The two are defined by their absolute heterogeneity – "there is no other example in the history of human thought of two categories of things so profoundly differentiated or so radically opposed to one another" (38). Sacred things tend to be isolated and protected by prohibitions, whereas profane things are those to which prohibitions apply and which must be kept separate from the sacred (40). According to Durkheim, totemic societies determine objects to be sacred by virtue of their closeness to a powerful being who represents the clan and with whom the clan identifies and treats as an external god (157). The totem god and its people are not in fact two distinct realities, but "the totemic principle must therefore be the clan itself, but transfigured and imagined in the physical form of the plant or animal species that serves as totems" (154). Thus, however distinct the totem's religious force is felt to be, it is in fact the collective and anonymous force of the clan.

The anonymous force of the totemic clan may be seen spectacularly when the group is not engaged in the profane activities of gathering, hunting, and fishing, but rather comes together in ecstatic corroboree. Then "[o]nce the individuals are assembled, their proximity generates a kind of electricity that quickly transports them to an extraordinary degree of exaltation ... The passions unleashed are so impetuous they cannot be contained" and may culminate in acts of violent transgression (2001: 162–163). Durkheim called such transports effervescence, wherein a people is transported to the world of the sacred, which leaves them convinced of the incompatibility of the worlds of the sacred and the profane (164).[44] Such experiences are always imminent. He pointed out that the very act of

---

[44] Described in Juergensmeyer and Kitts (2011:100–107).

assembling can promote a sense of rejuvenation, wherein the presence of the totem god is felt to be renewed (256).

On sacrifice, Durkheim distinguished the negative cult from the positive cult. The negative cult involves ascetic abstentions and prohibitions, wherein pain and suffering can be deemed transportive, as in Christian and other cults (2001:230–235). The positive cult seeks an exaggeration of the ordinary system of prohibitions. Although the sacred totem is less likely to be touched during positive cult experiences, members of those totemic cults that normally prohibit consuming the totem animal might on this occasion be permitted to consume it as a communal meal, but only after the animal has undergone a series of preliminary rites – washing, anointing, and the like. Relying on Robertson Smith, Durkheim saw totem meals as establishing kinship among a people and its god and the totem animal as giving this meal a sacred character (249). Since every member of the clan "bears within him a sort of mystic substance" tied to his soul and this, over time, can be felt to diminish, members will be inclined to renew and rejuvenate that mystic substance through the taking of the totem's flesh (250). There is an element of sacrilege in such consumption, but it is mitigated by ritual precautions.

Although there is little in his sacrificial theory that was not derivative from Robertson Smith, Durkheim is to be credited with his revolutionary hypothesis that the "sacred principle is nothing but society hypostasized and transfigured," and that ritual offers the gods not actually the material substance of blood or flesh or grain, but in fact the worshipper's thought. Sacred beings live only in human consciousness, he opined (2001:257). He thereby secularized the study of religion.

Hubert (1872–1927) and Mauss (1872–1950)

Henri Hubert and Marcel Mauss, two of Durkheim's students, harnessed Durkheim's division of religious experience into categories of sacred and profane by studying Vedic and biblical sacrifice. In *Sacrifice: Its Nature and Function* they asked how a sacrificial victim, whose role in ritual is to die, can offer a pathway to divinity and the sacred? Exploring the diversity of sacrificial practices particularly in Vedic thought, they established the basic pattern that every object of actual sacrifice passes from the profane to the sacred domain by being destroyed and thereby consecrated. The consecrated victim serves as an intermediary between the sacrifier (one on whose behalf the victim is offered) and the divinity to whom the sacrifice is usually addressed, via the activities and tools of the sacrificer (one who conducts the sacrifice).

Thus, in contrast to the totemic theories of sacrifice explored earlier, here in sacrificial rituals humans and gods are never in direct contact. Entry into the world of sacrifice is dangerous for the sacrifier. He must enter the sacred world to increase his own religiosity, and he must become associated closely with the victim who dies to confer this religiosity, but because the victim is to be killed, the sacrifier who is identified with the victim also risks a similar fate.

> He needs to touch the animal in order to remain united with it, and yet is afraid to do so, for in so doing he runs the risk of sharing its fate. The ritual resolves the difficulty by taking a middle course. The sacrifier touches the victim only through the priest, who himself only touches it through the intermediary of one of the instruments of sacrifice. Thus this process of drawing together the sacred and the profane, which we have seen come about progressively through the various elements of the sacrifice, is completed in the victim. (1968:52)

The entire process, however, is more complicated than a simple transport to and from the realm of the sacred via an intermediary. Sacrifices can have multidimensional functions. Hindu sacrifice, for instance, may commit shares of the animal to propitiate evil spirits, divine shares on one side, shares for communion on the other, and shares for priestly consumption on yet another. Not only is it a matter of shares; a victim may bring imprecations down on an enemy through sacrifice, may redeem a sacrifier for whatever trespass, and may even be deemed a substitute for the sacrifice of a god, as in the case of God Soma (1968:96). There are agrarian sacrifices meant to fertilize the earth, in contrast to personal sacrifices that might ensure the life of an individual (72–73). The unity among this multiplicity of purposes is the establishment of communication between the worlds of the sacred and the profane through mediation of a victim through its destruction (97).

If one may abstract from these descriptions, what Hubert and Mauss were formulating in brief was a theory of ritual dynamics. In contrast to Robertson Smith, who saw the victim as coming to the realm of sacrifice already sacred (via its totemic status), Hubert and Mauss saw the ritual itself as conferring this sacred status, which the victim then could pass on to the profane or the religious world as an intermediary (1968:97). It is arguable that by fixating on the ritual as the means of transporting the victim between sacred and profane realms, Hubert and Mauss anticipated some theories of the past half century that stressed the formalization of ritual as a means of heightening the register of communication (see, e.g., Fernandez 1977, Bloch 1989, Rappaport 1999, and others).[45] Mauss himself might be argued to have forecast these trends in his delightful "Techniques of the Body" (1973 [1935]), which articulated a theory of ritual "habitus," which then was picked up by the "lived religion school" (Vasquez 2011:241), among others.[46]

However, the theory has also been criticized for its reflexive adoption of Durkheim's sacred/profane dichotomy and the idea that sacrifice is somehow transportive. As Detienne pointed out, in Classical Greek culinary sacrifice "neither the sacrificer nor the victim is supposed to leave the world at any time" (1989:14); rather the practice of Olympian sacrifice reaffirmed the absolute break between the human and divine worlds and the cohesion among those dining on the victim (on the originary drama, see Vernant 1989:21–86).

Jensen (1899–1965)

Despite being steeped in the evolutionary arguments of his time, Adolf E. Jensen resisted unilineal evolutionary assumptions when it came to art, play, and the reputedly alien mentalities of early humans (1963 [1951]:35–38). Distinguishing technological advances from the sophistication of ideas, he denied that early human mentalities were fundamentally alien to

[45] For a summary, see Kitts 2018a:36–83. [46] Described in Kitts 2022.

us and strove to understand the creative cultural configurations that "archaic cultivators" produced. In fact, he argued, the primary obstacle to our understanding of primitive peoples is that they "possess a highly developed faculty for symbolic representation" that we tend to lack (186). The cultural configuration he strove to reconstruct was the practice of sacrificial killing lodged in the dema mythologem, which was associated with archaic root crop cultivators as found in Indonesia, New Guinea, and the Americas, and among some peoples of India (166–167). Although his *Myth and Cult of Primitive Peoples* accounted for a variety of ritual killings, including heroic killings seeded in honor codes and the mythic dynamics associated with the theft of cereal grains from sky gods, Jensen is most recognized for researching the dema mythologem associated with archaic root crop cultivators.

Jensen drew his dema hypothesis from the myth of Hainuwele, a primeval woman venerated by root crop cultivators of Ceram, New Guinea. Unlike Western high gods understood as historically omnipresent and omniscient, the dema-deity is understood to have come into temporal being on earth, to have once offered her people auspicious gifts, but then to have been murdered in a primal and violent past. Her murder set in play the contours of the contemporary age (1963[1951]:91); from her body originated root crop plants, the eating of which is in symbolic terms the eating of the deity (167). The dema were not initially identified with the deity; they were instead the primal beings who killed the deity, thereby ending the primal era, and who became men who were mortal and propagated kin. Henceforth the dema-deity, as Jensen called it, came to reside in the realm of the dead, but mortals continued to enjoy its gifts in the contemporary age.

Jensen was keen to distinguish the relatively contemporary practice of "sacrificing to" a god for the purpose of, say, rainmaking and encouraging the fertility of fields, dispelling the curse of barrenness, and so forth from the practice of ritual killing among archaic root crop cultivators. The former sacrifices were to be understood as semantically depleted survivals of an archaic and authentic religious impulse whose emotional resonance was more profound: the killing and eating of an animal among root crop cultivators was an intensified act of commemoration of the slaying and eating of the dema-deity (1963[1951]:172–173), this slaying being understood as the divine act from which all things stem (167). On one hand, this primordial act launches a virtual charter commemorated in all kinds of derivative celebrations, such as puberty rituals, death rituals, and harvest feasts (168). On the other, participation in the cultic rituals commemorating this slaying also could be a vehicle for inducing what Jensen, following Frobenius, called an *Ergriffenheit*, a seizure, an engulfment, a lifting of humans out of their customary realities to expose this dramatic originary moment, after which aspects of these experiences may get passed on didactically, which is to say in depleted form (4, 53, 56).

By today's standards Jensen's defense of this *Ergriffenheit* as the initiation of a primal awareness and vivid "knowledge" of the nature of reality, achieved through killing rites and ceremonies (1963[1951]:77), is perhaps the most progressive aspect of his thinking. In this he anticipated the sacrificial theories of Girard and Burkert, as well as the ritual theories of Whitehouse (2004), Alcorta and Sosis (2005), and others who explore ritual means of inducing profound awarenesses elusive to discursion.

Bataille (1897–1962)

Georges Bataille was a twentieth-century French intellectual whose theory of religion was based on his theory of economics as articulated in *The Accursed Share*. He compared societies to plants stimulated by the sun: they produce more beauty than is strictly needed for utility. By this paradigm, societies too produce surpluses of energy beyond strictly utilitarian needs and may be evaluated by how they spend this surplus energy. They spend it, in some circumstances, on religious spectacles and sacrifices, which are key to his evaluation of such societies.

In his *Theory of Religion* Bataille addressed the tension between the understanding of sacrificial animals as things to be used and eaten versus our suspicion of "immanence" when a priest is about to immolate the animal in sacrifice. Typically, he said, we distance ourselves from the animals we eat. By killing, cutting up, and eating an animal we define it as a thing for our use; its body was in fact a thing before we used it as such, when we planned to use it as such (2011:39). In contrast, we are repulsed from considering the same of a human body, or from doing anything utilitarian with it, as we implicitly suspect the human corpse to be the substratum of a spirit (40). Indeed, when death reduces the human body to a thing, we feel the spirit more acutely than ever, as if the corpse were haunted by it: its felt presence is intensified, at least for a moment, by its absence. "What death's definitive impotence and absence reveals [*sic*] is the very essence of the spirit, just as the scream of the one that is killed is the supreme affirmation of life" (40).

Immanence is felt when the sacrificial victim is drawn out from the things that are basically nothing to us, into a world that is intimate to us, when we and the victim are separated from the world of things and instead are felt to be immanent in the "sovereign world of gods and myths" (2011:44). This "divine world" is equated with the profound immanence of all that is (44); we participate in it, but "[i]ntimacy cannot be expressed discursively" (50). In this world of immanence distinctions such as death and life are not exactly distinctions; rather they seem to resolve into each other, as death is sensed as "the wonder-struck cry of life" (46). Death thus can illuminate the meaning of sacrifice, as if "restoring a lost value through a relinquishment of that value" (48). "When the offered animal enters the circle in which the priest will immolate it, it passes from the world of things which are closed to man and are nothing to him, which he knows from the outside – to the world that is immanent to it, *intimate*, known as the wife is known in sexual consumption" (45).

Therefore, although the principle of sacrifice is destruction, its intention is not actually to bring about annihilation; only the victim's thinghood is destroyed, as are individual identities of sacrificer-priests. Something more profound happens. Taking part in the killing during sacrifice, an "individual" is defined by anguish, by distress, because "[t]he individual identifies with the victim in the sudden movement that restores it to immanence (to intimacy), but the assimilation that is linked to the return to immanence is nonetheless based on the fact that the victim is the thing, just as the sacrificer is the individual" (2011:51) who kills the victim, returning it to the world of things. This is the ambiguity of sacrifice: it is both destructive of the thing and transformative in inducing one's sense of immanence with the victim destroyed.

Bataille's writing style reflects the surrealist influences of his youth in that it is elliptical and sometimes obscure. In its psychological description it broaches the kind of phenomenology we associate with Eliade, which is to say, a very loose phenomenology. It is certainly not anthropological or ethnological, as the theory is created out of Bataille's own musings. Nonetheless he remains philosophically important insofar as his ideas influenced a number of French thinkers, such as Foucault, Derrida, and Agamben.

Jay (1929–1991)

In *Throughout Your Generations Forever* (1992) sociologist Nancy Jay surveyed sacrificial practices in cultures as diverse as the Ashanti of Ghana and the native Hawaiians. From these studies she developed the "descent theory" of sacrifice, which argues that sacrificial rituals provide experiences of male bonding that privilege men in patrilineal societies. She based this conclusion on her analysis of two anthropological movements in ritualized blood sacrifice: *expiation* – eliminating unwanted elements as unclean – and *communion*, which integrates elements into a new whole. The expiated elements were typically matrilineal, such as a boy's natural descent from the mother. The communion element was a boy's initiation into the new kinship group, which was male-oriented and patrilineal. Focusing particularly on the Priestly (P) accounts of sacrifice in the Bible (Lev. 3:17, 10:19, 17:7, 23:31, 41, 24:3), she claimed that it is P who establishes male descent as primary "throughout your generations forever."

This explains why, in her view, not only the Bible but most sacrificial institutions prohibit female participation. Participation is viewed as an exclusively male privilege to be established when an initiate kills a victim. The killing forges a special bond between fathers and sons, and the son's new identity is seen as overcoming the chaos and destiny toward death that results from birth from the mother. Communion with the new exclusively male group not only expiates male descent from a woman but implicitly confers a kind of immortality, and thus sacrificial institutions are ways of transcending death, as well as ways of transcending natural birth. By ritually killing sacrificial victims, sacrificial societies secure symbolic rebirth and figurative immortality for men.

The Romans offer one model of the societies Jay examines, but the model transcends the Roman context. Here she distinguished cognation – descent relationships traced through both women and men – versus agnation, or patrilineal descent. The first tends to be very broad and difficult to trace through the generations, whereas the second is narrow and sedimented through sacrificial practices. Agnation gave Roman families and lineages a social continuity that was deemed eternal (1992:41–42), and allowed male citizens, who were defined by undergoing these rituals, to participate in civic institutions. Similarly with Nuer social structures all the way over in Africa: although cognation (*mar*) is more important in daily life than agnation (*buth*), participation in sacrifice establishes exclusively male social structures through the eating of meat. Jay translated *buth* as "to share the meat of sacrifice" (42). Similarly, she argued that the Tallensi and Lugbara establish lineage bonds through sacrifice (43). Jay was keen on showing that participation in these animal sacrifices was not preestablished by social organization and expressed in sacrifice, but rather the cult of sacrifice itself established these bonds through the ritualized sharing of the flesh of animal sacrifice.

However, Jay also showed that not every society was quite so straight-forward. In their heyday (seventeenth century) the Ashanti of present-day Ghana, for instance, kept royal matrilineal sanctuaries and, unlike some of their neighbors, were relatively egalitarian. Some of the social complexity was due to the mother's brother having authority over royal children, which could be a source of conflict with their father, who was able to handle the children of slaves and concubines as he wished, including offering them as human sacrifices or to slave traders. Despite their relatively egalitarian society the Ashanti practiced both human and animal sacrifice on a large scale, notably at an annual meeting where all the chiefs were expected to show allegiance to the king through their quotas of human sacrifices. A special patrilineal group, the executioners, were empowered to conduct these human sacrifices, which were understood to serve the ghosts of dead kings (1992:65–76). Although these sacrificial cults were well developed for male royalty, it is notable that never were sacrifices conducted for female royalty despite the existence of female royal sanctuaries. This is implied to support Jay's point about the patrilineal dimensions of sacrificial practices.

On the ancient Hawaiians, Jay drew on Valerio Valeri to explore their sacrificial system, which she saw as especially invested in a gendered hierarchy (1992:77–92). It should be noted, however, that that hierarchy was challenged more than two centuries ago when the Hawaiian *kapu* system was repudiated and, on the matter of gendered identities and responsibilities, it would be a historical blunder to see Hawaiian culture, then as now, as socially static, particularly given its powerful queens.

Overall, concerning the principle of patrilineal identities being established through sacrifice, especially in the ancient Mediterranean world, lacunae in our historical knowledge do not allow us to embrace Jay's thesis as a simple gendered matter, at least for Western antiquity. As Ruane points out, biblical texts do emphasize sacrifice as primarily a male endeavor, but it is not inconceivable that women had sacrificial roles that were minimized or even obfuscated by biblical authors, and the lack of conspicuous religious roles for women may be explained by childbearing obligations that interfered with, for example, undertaking pilgrimages (2013:21–29; see also Kramer 2004:9–11). In Classical Greek inscriptions and art women are shown as priestesses who offer sacrifices (Connelly 2007:179–190) and in literature they play roles as patriotic sacrificers of themselves or their children in heroic endeavors to save their cities. As Lefkowitz points out, these self-sacrifices should not be viewed as implying second-class status, and in tragedy, at least, are not represented as the slightest bit disparaging (2007:95–105). Suffice it to say that gender is not a stand-alone factor in some of these ancient sacrificial representations.

Girard (1923–2015)

Violence lies at the core of René Girard's sacrificial theory: "Violence strikes men as at once seductive and terrifying, never as a simple means to an end, but as an epiphany" (Girard 1977:152). Although an early point, this remains arguably his most important one, which he made while musing on the Greek god Dionysos and on the semidivine prestige of battlefield heroes in Homeric epic (143–168). There is nothing actually divine about the source of this epiphany; it is rooted in a fully human psychosocial urge he called mimetic desire. Mimetic desire is born when a rival lacks a fulfilling sense of "being," which he is certain that his rival possesses in abundance (146). This suspicion is contagious and, since we have no natural braking system to curb it (Mack 1987:8), the rivals will burst into acts of

violence, which can lead to larger cycles of reciprocal violence and ultimately to terrifying outbreaks of social anarchy and chaos. Without
a scapegoating diversion, these outbreaks can lead to societal collapse.
Fear of this collapse is the very spur for the creation of culture, said Girard.

To contain outbreaks of reciprocal violence, societies have devised
apotropaic rituals to rid themselves of innumerable and contagious mimetic
rivalries and to avoid outbursts of what Girard called "violent unanimity."
To deflect these outbursts, societies collectively target surrogate victims
with general resemblances to actual targets of mimetic rivalry (detailed in
his 1977 opus), and these become sacrificial substitutes, or scapegoats, killed
in controlled institutionalized settings. These killings induce a kind of
catharsis whereby the scapegoats absorb the uncontained mimetic rivalries
into themselves and thereby cleanse the society of its deep-seated violent
urges. It is typically (but not only) organized religion that, either by staging
ongoing rituals or by sacrificial ideology, confers a sanctified status to this
scapegoat, as it is only by the scapegoat's death that the society is cleansed.

The most significant attribute of the scapegoat is this religious
hallowing. When religion embraces the scapegoating impulse, the scapegoat is transformed by religious ideology into a relatable hero,
a savior who is killed to absolve us of our violent impulses.
Scapegoating generates not only peace but also reverence for the sacrificial victim whose killing has made peace possible. This leads to
Girard's most sensational point: all peaceful societies are founded on
the scapegoat's murder (Girard 2014b:2, 31–32) and all rules of culture
stem from the banding together of all against a single victim (Girard
1987:27). These are "things hidden since the foundation of the world"
(Girard 1987:143–149).

Girard's thinking was not without controversy. For one thing, he
became enamored with Christian theology over time, which shifted his
understanding of our propensity to violence. Girard vacillated between
figurative and literal readings of biblical texts, and even went so far as to
associate our disorderly disposition with an earth-bound Satan (2014a:54,
1987:162–163) and to link mimetic desire with the Christian notion of
original sin. In his view mimetic desire began with Adam and Eve but
broke into violent expression with Cain's murder of Abel: "The murder of

the brother, you see, is the creation of human culture. The whole mimetic system is there, and the Gospels say so" (2014b:31). It culminates, however, with the crucifixion of Christ. For Girard, the Gospels differed from other mythologies by revealing openly the cruel death of the innocent victim and by illustrating how that death unified spectators of all ranks (1987:163–170; 2011:67–68, 74; 2014b:28, 33–34). In Pauline terms Girard saw the crucified Christ as the last sacrifice, the scapegoat for sin, and the new Adam who freed us from the burden of further mimetic rivalries and scapegoating (2014b:31). Perhaps most remarkably, Girard came to see mimetic desire as potentially salvific in a Christian context – that is, when Christ is the model for the rivals. At that point he saw divine grace as present in mimetic desire: mimetic desire causes the disciple to open out onto the world (1996:62–65). When Christ is the model mimetic desire can eclipse the vicious tangle of rivalry and instead generate love. One constraint on this love generation is that it is out of reach for most people. Only Christ has ever equaled God in pure love (216).

This bleak picture, based on the evidentiary nature of the Bible, was jarring to critics, as was Girard's dichotomy of myth versus truth (the Gospels representing truth), his use of literature to construct anthropological claims, and his pinning of sacrificial conventions on a single base in mimetic desire (Kitts 2002:20). The theory is flawed also by a number of its psychological presumptions, not least among them the lack of interiority of the rivals, who are presented as incapable of checking their own aggressions. It is also flawed by its failure to explain love, which Girard confines to Christian *agapē* and models thereof. Theologically speaking, while in his later years Girard made mimetic rivalry not inevitably violence-inducing when the model for mimesis was Christ, this was a mystical mimesis. Overcoming mimetic rivalry was only possible because of altruistic love, which he saw as unattainable for anyone not exposed to Christ (and only Christ has ever equaled God in pure love, said Girard [1996:216]). In 2014, when pressed by Michel Tregeur, Girard admitted that parental love conceivably might be free of mimetic desire, but that love's expression was restricted: "The possibilities of the autonomous self are always hindered by mimetic desire and by a false individualism whose appetite for differences tends to have a leveling effect." He continued to maintain that all desire remained at core a desire for being (Girard 2014b:12), which mirrors one of his earliest points (1977:146).

Despite its flaws Girard's theory cast a far-reaching spell on popular thinking (see, e.g., Palaver 2021). His theory resonates with older arguments that religions shelter violent urges and ideologies in order to tame and channel them, as argued in, for example, Freud's *Totem and Taboo*. But obviously Girard's theory will not be able to explain sacrificial etiologies such as feeding the gods or replicating cosmovisions (as summarized in Section 1).

Burkert (1931–2015)

One theme Walter Burkert emphasized along with Girard was the epiphany induced by violence, although in his case it was the violence controlled in ritual sacrifice. His essential claim, as put forth in *Homo Necans* (1972, English transl. 1983), was that "sacrificial killing is the basic experience of the 'sacred'" and that "homo religiosus acts and attains self-awareness as homo necans" or "man the killer" (Burkert 1983:3). Unlike Girard, Burkert did not see this epiphany as stemming from a collective act of violent unanimity or scapegoating. Rather, he saw this epiphany as induced initially by the hunter's confrontation with an animal's death, an epiphany replicated in ritual sacrifice.

As a Classicist, Burkert traced this fascination with death in the ritual sequence of ancient Greek domestic animal sacrifice: for the Bouphonia, after a ceremonious procession to the altar, participants witnessed the peak moment when the victim, his throat slit, gasped for air as he clung to life for precious last seconds. His gasps and death rattle were muffled by women's high-pitched ritual screams, the screams marking the emotional climax of the event. In some cases, an inadvertent nod of consent was obtained from the victim before slaughter so as to assuage guilt at the killing and at the sight of the spilt blood, which appeared to participants to be as steaming and red as human blood, and just as representative of life. Although most ancient sacrifices ended in jubilation and feasting on meat (Burkert 1987:164) – not a staple in all ancient diets – Burkert saw at the very moment of the kill a root trauma based on emotional identification with the victim. Ritual sacrifice was a peak religious experience because in that dreadful and exhilarating moment of the kill we became aware of what it meant to live, that we thrived at the expense of another creature's death (Burkert 1983:38). He pointed out that we are the only carnivore to make a ritual out of killing and eating meat, and that no other religious experience can rival ritual sacrifice for arousing an intensity of feeling. Hence a number of well-known Greek myths – that is, the trick of Prometheus and the Titan sacrifice of Dionysos – betray an ancient ambivalence about it.

Aware that sacrificial practices have occurred on all continents deep into history, Burkert in his early works searched for the roots of ritual killing in our paleolithic heritage as hunter-gatherers. Basing his theory on man as the hunting ape, Burkert in 1972 sought to pin the difference between other primates and human primates on the *Männerbund*, the male hunting band that developed as part of our evolution from peaceful and vegetarian apes into an aggressive band of carnivores. Initially Burkert relied on studies by Karl Meuli that tied Neanderthal burials of bears to Siberian hunters' burial rituals and to "comedies of innocence" reminiscent of the aforementioned Greek Bouphonia ("ox-murder"), where the bones and skin of the sacrificed ox were "resurrected" and guilt for the killing was assigned to the culpable ax – tried and exiled for murder. Such comedies of innocence, according to Meuli, betrayed "an underlying anxiety about the continuation of life in the face of death" (Burkert 1983:16) or a "memorable manifestation of pity" (Meuli, in Burkert 2013:441–442). Meuli's theories have since been challenged: newer studies find simple societies wherein no remorse at all is demonstrated when animals are butchered for food, which begs us to consider the diversity of human societies and the difficulty of trying to reconstruct the emotions of early humans, as Burkert himself noted (2013:442). As for our shared emotional repertoire with apes, newer ethological studies have uncovered occasional murders, cannibalism, and even group battles in some ape societies (Burkert 1987:163–64), although others argue that these animal societies are hardly pristine, given the likely effects of the gaze of contemporary researchers (Ferguson 2006; Kitts 2018a:26–36). However, evidence of hunting ceremonies, animal corpse markings, and animal burials among paleolithic hunter-gatherers still is enlisted to support Burkert's basic theory about the ambivalence felt in animal killing among early humans, and indirectly supports possible ritual inducements for group bonding such as the reputed male bonding experience cemented in the simultaneous exhilaration and remorse of killing big, humanlike game. According to Burkert, a constellation of exhilaration and remorse over thousands of years (since *Homo erectus* [Burkert 2013:442]), indelibly imprinted human nature so as to become a sought-after experience of the sacred, eventually expressed in the ritual sacrifice of domesticated animals. The neolithic revolution is responsible for the transformation from hunt to sacrifice: once agriculture and animal husbandry eliminated the need for hunting big game, the exhilaration and remorse that once unified the male hunting band sought communal expression in the staged sacrifice of friendly, domesticated animals and in other culturally sanctioned rituals of violence.

In 1972 Burkert explained the bonding effects of ritualized killing in terms of animal rituals. Citing the ethological studies of Konrad Lorenz, Burkert saw ritual as essentially a form of communication that was theatrically exaggerated. Lorenz's famous example was the greylag geese whose triumph ceremony has ceased to communicate alarm about or victory over opponents but now serves as a dance geese pairs perform to communicate and identify with each other and to announce their identification as a pair to other members of the group. The dance still can be used to signify ritual hierarchy (triumph) and submission; even among geese, ritual communication is polyvalent. Humans too practice rituals that communicate, innate ones such as smiling, laughing, and crying, but also staged ones, such as animal sacrifice. Burkert compared sacrifice to an excited ritual display of aggression that communicates solidarity among the group and dramatizes the existing social order (1983:24–25). It too once had concrete survival value in the great hunt for meat and now serves other social functions. Although different rationales may be offered for the performance of a particular ritual, according to Burkert the attraction of ritual is far older than its culturally specific rationale, and its communicative effects are more profound (1996).

Burkert's theories have triggered whole schools of critics. Some have challenged Burkert's evolutionary paradigm and his trust in Konrad

Lorenz's theory of aggression. As with any theory that posits deep impulses
that elude everyday awareness, the hunting trauma hypothesis must persuade by eliciting such an awareness, particularly as the empirical data are
ambiguous; some critics fail to recognize what Burkert would elicit. Others
criticize his assumption of gender dichotomies (see Jay 1992), for which he
also offers an evolutionary explanation (1972). On the hunting ritual
evoking a primordial trauma, the hunting ceremonies of circumpolar
peoples, presumably maintaining a relatively untainted continuity for generations, show a great variety of relationships to their prey. Some do
idealize an animal-human co-sociality, which betrays a seeming anxiety,
as when Nordic hunters claim to sing animals into surrendering to death;
others willfully deceive pet bear cubs raised for sacrifice, showing little if
any remorse (Willerslev, Vitebsky, and Alekseyev 2015). While studies of
existing hunter-gatherers do not completely prove or disprove Burkert's
notion of an ontic seizure at the spectacle of killing, they do support the
"double bind" (Bateson 1972:271–278) between the idealized and pacific
hunt in which the animal colludes in its killing, versus the messy reality of
tracking and killing victims. This double bind is suggested by some Nordic
anthropologists to have been "a key motivator in transforming the actual
hunt into the highly controlled pattern of ritual blood sacrifice" (Willerslev
et al. 2015:10).

J. Z. Smith (1938–2017)

Some of these ideas were tackled by the historian of religion Jonathan
Z. Smith, who was well known as a critic of the "big theories" of religious
sacrifice. For instance, against Jensen's *Ergriffenheit* or the primal ambivalence of Burkert's *Männerbund*, Smith pointed to a variety of understandings
of the hunter's experience, contrasting urban agricultural societies that
might romanticize the hunter as facing the realm of wild animals as
a threat, as chaos, or as death (e.g., as symbolized in the lion hunting rituals
of Mesopotamian royal art), versus actual hunting societies wherein hunting
is an everyday activity. In the latter case it is likely not perceived as an act of
overcoming but as participation in the normal course of things (1982:57–58;
2004:148). He also pointed out that there was no evidence of paleolithic
hunters' ritual sacrifice; nearly all cases of sacrifice on record stem from

agricultural societies that sacrifice domesticated animals and for which ritual killing is reduced to the art of the selective kill, rather than the hunters' fortuitous kill (2004:148–149, 153–155). For those who actually sacrifice animals, it is a matter of animal husbandry rather than an ontic seizure (1987).

In "Bare Facts of Ritual" (1982) Smith reported studies of those few societies that do engage in hunting rituals, namely Nordic hunting societies that postulate rather extraordinary roles and rituals relating to the bear hunt. One role is that of a "Master of Animals," understood to control game or their spirits and to release an allotted number to be hunted for food. The mythology of the hunt allows that the soul of each animal must be returned to its supernatural owner by ritual means. If the system is violated, ritualized ceremonies must remove any offense.

The other sets of rituals Smith broke down into four. First are rituals that prepare hunters for a successful hunt (e.g., divination, ceremonies depicting sympathetic magic, purification of the hunter). These include training in ceremonial hunt language wherein euphemisms and circumlocutions are addressed to the animal in order to persuade it to succumb to the hunter, but also to obscure the hunter's killing intention. Second are departure rituals that suggest that the hunter is leaving the prescribed order of human social structures for the forest's domain and must be given permission to enter as a guest of the host-forest. The hunted animal is understood as a gift from the spirit world where abides the Master of Animals; the animal too is seen as a host to the hunters as they feed on its flesh. There is some reciprocity, as by killing and eating an animal hunters can return its essence to its supernatural owner (1982:59). Third is the kill, also embedded in a system of etiquette, such as the aforementioned verbal persuasion as well as the necessity of killing the animal in hand-to-hand, face-to-face combat and never while it is asleep in its den. There are rules for where the bear can and cannot be wounded (as bloodlessly as possible). Following the kill is a disclaimer of responsibility recited over the corpse. Either the animal fell on the weapon or was killed by weapons from foreigners; the disclaimers may be creative (59–60). Last is the strategic retreat, when the hunters leave the forest domain and return to the human, while carrying the corpse in solemn procession and reminding the animal that its soul may now return to its supernatural owner. There are also purification ceremonies for the hunters reentering the domestic world and rules about who may eat the animal's flesh and how it is divvied up to reflect the social map. Bones may play important roles, as bones are where the animal's generic life resides. These return elements were commemorated in the forty-sixth rune of the Finnish Kalevala.

Of these hunting rituals, Smith asked some blunt questions, which were inferred in the earlier discussion of Willerslev and colleagues. Smith asked if we seriously are to believe that the animal is mesmerized by the hunter's "dithyrambs," ceremonial addresses, and even love songs. Can a bear be killed bloodlessly and in face-to-face combat? Is it likely that the hunter who has in fact killed by stealth and skill will view the killing as an unfortunate accident and not boast about it? (1982:61). For Smith, historians of religion need to investigate alternative hypotheses.

For instance, in recent studies of the Koryak and Chukchi, it turns out that these Nordic bear hunters have added a shotgun to their arsenal, which rather diminishes the likelihood of hand-to-hand combat. They also use traps and snares, self-triggering bows, and other tools that preclude much of the hunting etiquette previously summarized. One group who espouses not surprising a bear but rather having a fair, stand-up fight in fact ambushes the bear by a spearhead covered with spikes and attached to a cord that the hunter causes to be raised so as to impale the animal (1982:61). A notable problem with reconciling the ideology and actuality of the bear hunt lies in the bear's unlikely willingness to participate in the ritual etiquette; thus the hunter must cultivate other strategies to capture and kill the bear for food. The incongruity between how the hunter says he sees what he is doing and how he in fact hunts leads us to ask how hunters resolve this incongruity, as they surely see it just as we do and have cultivated a certain skill at rationalization (62).

After exploring a few similar incongruities among hunters on different continents, Smith suggested that a major function of ritual is to "represent the creation of a controlled environment where the variables of ordinary life are displaced precisely because they are felt to be so overwhelmingly present and powerful" (1982:63). Thus, in tension with the way things ought to be (the ritualized etiquette of the hunt) is the way things are in fact (the bear is an unwilling partner to the etiquette), so that "*this ritualized perfection is recollected in the ordinary, uncontrolled course of things*" (63; italics in the original text). Although he didn't use Bateson's concept of the double bind, Smith did report what he called a "gnostic" dimension to ritual. "Ritual provides an occasion for reflection and rationalization on the fact that what ought to have been done was not done [but relies] for its power on the perceived fact that, in actuality, such possibilities cannot be realized . . . Ritual gains force where incongruency is perceived and thought about" (63). So we may take from this that the ritualized niceties serve to highlight the disparity between the ideal hunt and the actual one, and that this disparity provides a certain tension that informs the ritual's meaning for its practitioners.

In 2004 Smith again focused on the elaborate, highly formalized rules of ritual sacrifice and suggested that its ritual dimensions were deliberate exaggerations, that "*in its agrarian or pastoral context, [sacrifice] is the artificial (i.e., ritualized) killing of an artificial (i.e. domesticated) animal*" (2004:152; italics in the original text). It is thus a meditation on one cultural process (killing animals for food) by means of another (exaggerating its ritual dimensions), similarly to the hunting rituals that provide an occasion for reflecting on what was not done in the face of what was. Paraphrasing Lévi-Strauss, Smith quipped that the sacrificial animals of agriculturalists are "goods to eat" and "goods to think" (2004:153).

Vernant (1941–2007) and Detienne (1935–2019)

The post-structuralists Jean-Pierre Vernant and Marcel Detienne criticized predominating theories of sacrifice from a classical Greek perspective. Arguing against universalizing theories, the post-structuralists rejected the anthropological category of sacrifice as overly comprehensive at best, as an artifact of Christian religion extended to non-Christian contexts at worst. It was not that sacrifices did not occur in ancient societies, but our ability to grasp their significances tended to be skewed by Europe's Christian heritage. Arguing against essentialist theories, Detienne pointed out that, as opposed to the universalizing ritual syntax that Hubert and Mauss drew from Vedic sacrifice – where the sacrifier (one on whose behalf the ritual is conducted) is reputed to vicariously transmigrate from the mundane world to the sacred and back again through the killing of an animal – the Greek sacrificer never leaves the world at any time. Instead he (and, yes, it was largely a he) remained firmly rooted in the complex of cultural codes that distinguished mortal existence from that of the immortal gods.

On comparativism, whereas Burkert saw the very study of Greek religion as comparative – the ancient Greek tradition spans a thousand years – the French structuralist school neglected the diachronic perspective for a synchronic one. They argued that studying the semiotic map of cultural codes in Greek literature and religion divulged a very broad landscape of Greek imagination, which, following Lévi-Strauss, they conceived as offering "a bundle of relations" whose overall sense was embedded in the arrangement of its parts, or codes. Each code had multiple echoes (Vernant 1989:24) that reverberated over this landscape and were amplified or muffled at various sites. Thus Greek sacrificial myth

> has no more one particular essence than a single detail of
> a myth is significant on its own. Every god is defined by
> a network of relations which links him with and opposes him
> to the other deities included within a particular pantheon;
> and similarly, a single detail is only significant by virtue of
> its place within the ordered system to which the myth itself
> belongs. (Vernant 1978:ix)

The constellation of legends that defined and cross-defined Greek *thysia* (commensal sacrifice) was described in the section on Greek sacrifice, but may be revisited briefly here. Hesiod's Prometheus myth established the rupture between gods and humans in the trickery of Titan Prometheus, who reserved the best portion of a sacrificial ox for humans during a divine-human feast we once enjoyed at Mecone. The gods were given bones wrapped in fat. In retaliation Zeus hid fire from humans, but Prometheus stole it for us and earned himself terrible punishment on our behalf, while we suffered punishment by our estrangement from the gods, but also by the gift of woman, the "beautiful evil" to match the blessing of fire (Th. 585).

Now men practice agriculture to raise food for themselves and their offspring and for the animals they sacrifice to the gods, sending pleasing
aromas up to the heavens and thereby establishing a faux divine-human
commensality that we in fact have lost (Vernant 1989:21–86).

As described earlier, Porphyry's account of the Athenian Bouphonia is
on one hand quite dire, although also conceivably comic in a tongue-in-
cheek way. The etiology is the "murder" (*phonē*) of the innocent plowing
ox (*bous*) caught munching cereal offerings for Zeus. When an angry
farmer struck the ox dead with an ax and buried the ox (thereafter fleeing
in self-imposed exile), his blood guilt brought on famine, which was
resolved by the Delphic oracle. Citizens were instructed to resurrect the
ox by effigy, invite the killer to return and kill it again with their help,
and dine upon it, thereby ritually replacing the act of ox-murder with ox-
sacrifice (a pun on the name Bouphonia). The ox meat was enjoyed by
the community and the ax was exiled for murder. For some scholars, such
a "comedy of innocence" betrays an anxiety about animal sacrifice, as
discussed earlier.

A third strand of legends also rejects animal sacrifice as murder.
Empedocles' fifth-century BCE theory of metempsychosis denied that
animals were lesser beings appropriate for sacrifice, since animal souls and
human souls were not only equal but interchangeable. After death animal
souls transmigrated into humans and vice versa. To sacrifice an animal
therefore was to risk committing murder, even conceivably of one's
deceased relatives.[47] To avoid this sort of filicide, said Empedocles,
Greeks ought to foreswear animal sacrifice. Pythagoras too is said to have
avoided sacrifices and eating meat, although the oral traditions about him
are ambiguous. He also is said to have embraced the theory of the transmigration of souls, as did, equally ambiguously, the Orphics.[48]

Detienne saw this refusal to participate in commensal sacrifices as
based on a refusal to endorse the notion that gods could be sought
through ritual bloodshed and a refusal to accept the rupture between
gods and men stemming from Hesiod's story of the fall. Instead, some

[47] Emped. fr. B 137 D-K. T, quoted in Naiden (2020:484).
[48] On both see https://plato.stanford.edu/entries/pythagoras.

Pythagoreans are said to have offered Apollo Genetor only nuts, spices, and grains that the earth spontaneously provided, as these were understood as the shared repast humans enjoyed with the gods before animal sacrifice entered human experience (Detienne 1994:44–47). At the other extreme of this virtuous vegetarianism are legends of dismemberment and homophagy associated with Euripides' Bacchantes, who reputedly challenged the suppositions of civic sacrifice by behaving as animals who tore and devoured their meat raw, under the spell of Dionysos. As Vernant and Detienne saw it, all of these legends interwove a whole text of interpretive codes reflecting right diet, agriculture, animal husbandry, butchery, cuisine, social dynamics of cuisine, divine-human dynamics of cuisine, and golden age memories versus the harshness of life now with its labor, marriage, illness, and death.

The theory has been criticized in several ways. Grottanelli observed, for instance, that any twentieth-century synchronic lens on Greek mythology was inevitably particularizing (1988), in response to which Vernant argued that the hermeneutic distortion that plagues all interpretation is minimized when Europeans study the Greeks because they are not as foreign to Europeans as others are. We can grasp the Greek mythic text because the Greek texts are reputedly transmitted to European scholars without a loss of continuity (Zeitlin 1991:7), which is an astonishing surrender of historical perspective considering the twenty-eight hundred years from Hesiod to us. Another critique regarded applying the Lévi-Straussian conception of culture as text to the whole of ancient Greek culture. One apparent disadvantage of the model, according to Geertz, is "the surface dissimilarity of the here-we-are-and-there-we-are of social interaction to the solid composure of lines on a page," although the model also can be advantageous when the "disaccordance is rightly aligned" (2000[1983]:31). Similarly, Ricoeur pointed out that nobody actually interprets a myth as a formal bundle of relations, like an algebra of constitutive units (1973:112). Instead, to understand a text, its depth-semantics, is to transcend the inscribed noema of the author's intention to get to what the text was about, its reference in the world (114). In any case, when we read we conjoin our own discourses to the one inscribed in the text so that, however perspectival our own discourse, that conjoining initiates novel ways of seeing the world (1981:158). Thus we needn't be entirely enclosed within the European worldview to understand, for instance, Empedocles' refusal to support what he understands as a broken relationship with the gods. Last, on the gendered dichotomy that Detienne argues excludes women from Greek blood sacrifice (1989), ancient testimonies establish that women were active in all aspects of Greek ritual sacrifice (Connelly 2007; Pirenne-Delforge 2007, and see earlier discussion of Jay), so this part of the theory is thoroughly debunked.

De Heusch (1927–2012)

In *Sacrifice in Africa* (1985) Luc de Heusch studied the great variety of relationships to animals as well as sacrificial practices between various African cultural groups, and the analyses of sacrifice by established scholars working with different cultural legacies. Despite his breadth of sacrificial study, he was particularly impressed with the structuralist approach to Greek sacrifice of Vernant and Detienne, described earlier, and he sought to distinguish the structures of conjunctive versus disjunctive sacrifices. Two themes he emphasized were the sacrificial meal and the sacrificed god-king.

On sacrificial meals, in contrast to Vernant and Detienne's horizontal commensality among Greek mortals versus the vertical and imagined commensality between mortals and Olympian immortals, the Mofu, Zulu, and Thonga peoples sacrifice an animal to establish commensality among the human family, with the ancestors understood as participating around the domestic hearth. As de Heusch sees it, there is no perceived gulf between people and the invisible realm, no Promethean trick that separates our realms forever, but rather the lineage community tightens its bonds with the dead through a shared meal. There is a variety of dietary rules – for example, who is allowed to roast the ancestors' share and where, although when that ancestral zone is outside of the living community, the lineage communion might seem less secure (1985:207). Further, there is some variation on the sacrificial etiology, pending group, as we see with the Nuer and Lugbara sacrifices. These are understood as debt repayments. In the Lugbara case this debt involves the sacrifier's entire lineage; the raw part goes to the ancestors, the cooked to the Lugbara men. The Nuer do not actually offer any meat to the spirits, but instead offer chyme, chyle, and blood – there is no alimentary communion and the territory of the ancestors or air spirits here too is separated from human territory. In yet another etiology the Massa perform sacrifice to drive away a threatening spirit. A dangerous heat that penetrates the body of the sacrificer passes into the victim, whose blood is a "cooling vector" (de Heusch 1985:208–209) that allows evil to escape. Here "the ancestors and the supernatural powers, fuliana, feed on blood and seek to make men die so as to satisfy their urges" (209). The ancestors thus are not welcome visitors, but dangerous ones. Here is where de Heusch distinguishes conjunctive sacrifices, as we saw with the Zulu and Mofu peoples seeking commensality with ancestors, from disjunctive, as we see among the Lugbara and Massa, who would drive away dangers through sacrifice.

As for royal sacrifices, de Heusch claimed to be a resolute Frazerian (1985:98–99) in maintaining that the sacred king, at least among some African groups, was condemned to die prematurely, to be ritually killed as part of his fate. Here too there was a great variety of traditions and etiologies across Africa. Broadly speaking, the king's monstrous countercultural nature was understood as inviting prohibitions against his excessive power. His body was both within and outside of cultural boundaries, he was surrounded by ritual interdictions, and incest and unnatural births formed a part of the royal landscape. In some cases instead of sacrificing the king a substitute was offered: a special animal or even a sickly human or war captive was killed (98–124). In one anthropophagous case among the Minyaka of Mali, the king's substitute, in this case a dog, was eaten by Nya initiates, who were understood as a kind of collective royal body. For their own safety, the initiates underwent a special purification beforehand. In contrast, among the West African Dogon, whose legends de Heusch describes in detail (125–160), only the impure could eat the goat, which represented the ancestor Lebe who was killed during a sowing festival. Lebe's flesh was dangerous due to his own storied transgressions. Ultimately for the Dogon the eating of the animal's flesh implied theophagy, as every Dogon sacrifice reenacted the birth and death of a different god, Nommo, humankind's divine ancestor and substitute offering in punitive place of the mischievous god Ogo, who was Nommo's twin brother. "[T]he immolation of a god makes reparation for the disorder that a rebellious creature, hungry for power and knowledge, brought into the universe when he prematurely tore himself loose from the original placenta, an act that threatened to make future humanity incomplete" (198). The legends are indeed creative and layered but also, in this case, grave and remedial for some kind of trespass. In the view of de Heusch at its base sacrifice was seen as a necessary attempt to outwit death, with human sacrifice at the outer limit of what was acceptable (215).

Because of the breadth of traditions summarized, it is difficult to imagine persuasive scholarly critiques of de Heusch. The structuralist approach seems a bit labored but the approach disappears behind the remarkable legends and practices he collected from within African traditions. *Sacrifice in Africa* remains ethnographically fascinating.

3 Controversies: "Sacrificial" Scenes in the *Iliad*

As suggested at the start of this Element, the big-picture accounts of sacrifice have lost favor in scholarly circles since specialists have taken up the challenge of asking what precisely sacrifice means for particular peoples and literatures. Despite the wide practice of sacrifice, the grand universalizing theories, even those that were appealing a few decades ago, now fall short. An example of the failure of universalizing theories to explain ritual sacrifice may be seen in their inability to capture the meanings of the starkly contrasting scenes of Homeric *thysia* (commensal sacrifice) versus *horkia* (oath-making sacrifice), as represented in the *Iliad*. To appreciate these contrasting scenes, first we need some background about the oral composition of the classical Greek poem and the way its ritual sacrifices are presented.

The poem of the *Iliad*, composed of 15,693 verses in dactylic hexameter, is thought to be the end product of centuries of flexible bardic performances on both sides of the Aegean Sea.[49] It is thought to have assumed its current

[49] For a summary, see Kitts 2015, but also short summaries of the unitarian versus analyst perspectives by West (2011a, 2011b). A summary of the problems with timing the composition of the Homeric *Iliad* is offered by Cairns (2001). It is a rich field.

shape as early as the eighth century BCE (Bryce 2006; but cf. Nagy 1990), but contains references to material elements – for example, silver-inlaid shields and shields so large that they resemble towers – traceable to the Bronze Age.[50] Although the poem is presumed to be a composite of different historical referents, based on comparative Near Eastern ritual conventions we may presume some degree of verisimilitude between the Homeric ritual scenes and actual Near Eastern rituals, particularly for *horkia* (oath-making scenes), but also for the occasional *thysia*-like scenes of dining, at least among the Hittite gods of Bronze Age Anatolia (described in Kitts 2011). The two sacrificial scenes vary in sequence, tone, and purpose but share features of Homeric typical scenes generally in that they are characterized by a density of repeated phrasing (relative to scenes of conversations or battles), as well as by unique rhythms and vocabularies. These unique phrasings, rhythms, and vocabularies are what accounts for their designations as typical scenes and, as has been argued elsewhere, suggest the great antiquity of the conventions they formalize in poetic representation (Kitts 2011, 2015). Examining this evidence from the origins of Western antiquity will allow us to observe some problems with presuming universalizing theories to adequately explain either *thysia* or *horkia* sacrifice.

Thysia: *Commensal Sacrifices*

The five *thysia* sacrifices in the *Iliad* reflect a common pace and patterning of food preparation and culminate with a feeling of satiation, denoted by the transitional verse "but when they had sated their desire for food and drink" (1:469; identical at 2:432, 7:323; 9:222; 24:628). Although the five scenes differ in degree of detail, the fullest scene (1:447–469) shows fifteen discernible, successive moments that together may be taken as a representative *thysia* ritual. That sacrifice is described with twenty-five finite verbs (discounting the prayer to Apollo) constituted by a ratio of nineteen aorists to

---

[50] On the images see Salimbetti at www.salimbeti.com/micenei/shields1.htm. Richard Janko (1992) discusses some Bronze Age material evidence. Diachronic versus synchronic examinations of the poem yield different scenarios for dating, as outlined in "Anthropology and the *Iliad*" (Kitts 2015).

six imperfects and two participles, all in only fifteen verses. By all the verbs we can see *thysia* scenes as bustling events that convey a burst of activity: these are busy scenes describing the preparing of and dining upon meat.[51] Another outstanding feature of *thysia* scenes is the total lack of reference to the victims' struggles or deaths, even though a full hecatomb of bovine is slaughtered in the sacrifice for Apollo in Book 1.[52]

What we hear instead is that participants swiftly set up a hecatomb of cattle around the altar (1:447–448), wash their hands, and take up barley (1:449). The priest Chryses prays, holding up his hands (1:450), asking Apollo to lift his curse from the Achaians (1.451–457) in the form of the plague he imposed on them for their earlier mistreatment of the priest and his daughter. The god hears (1.457). After this the participants pray, presumably for the same thing, and throw barley (1.458), apparently at the victim (although this is unstated). Next they hold up the victim's head, slaughter it, and flay it, all in one verse (1:459). The specialized slaughtering

---

[51] To give readers a sense of what is signaled by this relatively fixed cluster of verbs and participles marking commensal scenes, let us note that killing scenes, according to advocates of the theory of composition by single words, typically are quite fluid. They are built around a semantic nucleus denoting "X killed Y" – subject, indicative verb, object, plus a mandatory conjunction – and these tend to be localized in the initial part of the verse. But then there is a remarkable prosodic variety in the rest of the verse, specifying, for instance, whose son is the victim, where he is struck, what strikes him, how he dies or bereaves his parents. These might be comprised of any variety of supplementary participles and instrumental datives and can extend for verses beyond the killing nucleus. The peripheral expressions, according to this theory, represent details semantically inessential to the act of killing and show that the poet was able to compose with great lexical freedom in killing scenes (Visser 1988; Bakker and Fabricotti 1991). These are to be contrasted to ritual scenes, which tend to be more formalized.

[52] Cf. the *Odyssey*'s very developed sacrificial scene of Book 3, wherein a loss of strength (*menos*) on the part of the ox after it is struck is noted: "the strength of the ox loosened" λῦσεν δὲ βοὸς μένος (3.450), and then, after its blood runs out, its "*thumos* (spirit) left its bones" (λίπε δ᾽ ὀστέα θυμός) (3.455). There is nothing like this acknowledgment of death in the *thysia* scenes of the *Iliad*, which is generally accepted as the earlier poem.

verb here is *spha̧dō*, which implies cutting the throat (see earlier discussion of Greek sacrifice), although the throat itself is not mentioned. Then thigh pieces are cut out, covered in two folds of fat (1:460–461); raw strips of flesh are laid over the thigh pieces (1:461). The old man burns these over split wood and pours a libation of wine (1:462–63) – based on parallels in the *Odyssey* it is assumed that these meat bits and libations are for the god. Holding forks, young men stand by (1:463); they burn the thighs and taste the innards (1:464) while the rest is cut into bits, skewered with spits (1:465), and roasted expertly. The meat is drawn off (1:466), after which they cease their labor and prepare the feast (1:467). This is followed by a verse that is iconic for the satiation of the feast: "they feasted, and no spirit went lacking the equally divided feast" (1:468). Of this sequence, exactly ten verses are identical between at least two of the five commensal scenes, the last verse appears in all five and there are variations on the number of parallels in the others, with close matches especially for verses reporting the actual flaying, cutting, skewering, and roasting (Kitts 2011). These are indeed typical scenes.

One may see this pattern as both reified and abstract. It is reified by its concrete detail, micro-precision, and repeatability, as well as by the verses that express satiety – clearly the ultimate point of *thysia*. Yet the scene is also partially abstract because in all five commensal scenes the victims' blood and dying are ignored. Considering that the scene in Book 1 involves one hundred large mammals, the bloodlessness can only be a poetic fiction,[53] as must be the lack of attention to the victims' resistance while dying (cf. the bellowing oxen at the pre-funeral feast of Patroklos at 23:30–34[54]). These fictions serve to highlight the bustle and gratification

---

[53] Cf. *Odyssey* 3:455, where the blood gushes out into a bowl held for the purpose (3.444).

[54] Many glistening oxen bellowed around the iron as they were
slaughtered, and many sheep and bleating goats;
many white-toothed swine teaming with fat
being singed were stretched across the flame of Hephaistos;
all around the corpse ran blood that could be caught in cups. (23.30–34)
[translation by author]

of preparing food and dining and to cloak its painful aspects, if indeed any were felt.

Let us try to apply our universalizing theories to *thysia* sacrifices for a moment. Clearly these scenes cannot be assessed as befitting the primal trauma theories of Burkert, Girard, Freud, or indirectly Jensen. No one clearly identifies with the animal or is distressed about its killing, a lack of distress presumably implied in the three-verb verse indicating quick butchery: they hold up the victim's head, slaughter it, and flay it, all in one verse (1:459). The animal is pelted with barley – for Burkert an initial act of aggression (1983:5) – reportedly to achieve its nod of consent, yet this nod too is unstated. If there is any violence at all, it is not noted, making these violence-embracing theories seemingly beside the point.

Totemic theories are plausible, but by a stretch of the imagination, as only the priest Chryses is seen as having a conspicuous personal relationship with the god, as the god responded to him directly (1:457). Even so the priest shows no apparent relationship with the sacrificial victims, as in the three-way brotherhood of man-god-victim noted by Robertson Smith, Durkheim, Freud, and even Frazer. The Achaians may be presumed as also in relationship with Apollo since he has just lifted from them his punishing plague but, again, there is no sense that they share a brotherhood with the animals, even though the animals belonged to the Achaians (1:430–431).[55] The sacrifice is expected to reestablish a fellowship with the god and the people, as befitting the totemic theory in a general sense (Robertson Smith's, Durkheim's, even Frazer's), but this analysis does not seem to capture very much. Narrative context would appear to mitigate the power of these theories, particularly considering the conspicuous absence of Achilles, who has just refused to support commensal or any

See Kitts 2011 and 2008. For alternative translations for the word "bellowing" (*orechtheon*), see Liddell and Scott (1968: 1248).
www.perseus.tufts.edu/hopper/morph?l=o%29re%2Fxqeon%26la=greek%26can=o%29re%2Fxqeon0%26prior=a)rgoi\%26d=Perseus:text:1999.01.0133:book=23:card=1%26i=1#lexicon

[55] Cf. the ox in *Odyssey* 3, whose horns are gilded for the occasion (3.437–438). This presumably indicates at least a temporary focus on the victim.

other Achaian institutions. This absence hangs over the sacrificial narrative of Book 1 and diminishes the joyous unity presumed for this feast.

As for the theory of Hubert and Maus, the sacrificing beneficiaries might be understood as in rapport with Apollo, and the priest and the others do touch the animal by holding up its head and slicing its throat. Recall that touching the animal achieves a connection, per Hubert and Mauss (1964:52). Recall also that Detienne criticized Hubert and Mauss, claiming that humans in the Classical period remain firmly entrenched in the system of dietary codes that defines mortal existence as opposed to immortal; there is reputedly no sense that they transcend this domain for another one. Is the same true here, though, in this poem reputedly committed to its current iteration in the eighth century BCE rather than in the Classical period, which typically is held to begin at the end of the sixth century? It is notable that the establishment of a connection with the divine is expected, given Apollo's consent secured by Chryses' prayer. To this limited degree the theory of Hubert and Mauss might fit the context. The pleasure of the feast, however, would appear to be the outstanding theme here; the god's role is only briefly noted: "So he said, praying, and Phoibos Apollo heard him" (1:457).

As for the other theories, if there is anything like J. Z. Smith's "gnostic" aspect to the sacrifice, it is unstated, as the participants all appear to take the sacrifice at face value; there is no apparent mythological cloak behind the feast, except insofar as Apollo is expected to care about it. Because of its formality as a ritual scene and the absence of animal distress, we are missing anything like intimacy between the animal victim and sacrificer, per Bataille's theory. As for gendered aspects to the sacrifice, this is a war poem of Greek antiquity, so exclusively male participants are to be expected, given what we presume about ancient warfare.[56] Jay's theory that sacrifices expiate some conditions (Achaian guilt) and create new ones (cleansing) might be argued to apply loosely, but no obvious patrilineal identity is established and no matrilineal origins are erased; there is just shared good cheer. As for de Heusch, the only pertinent statement he makes is that at its base sacrifice is seen as a necessary attempt to outwit death, with

[56] Cf. Adrienne Mayor on Iron Age warrior women (2015).

human sacrifice at the outer limit of what was acceptable (1985:215). It is hard to argue with this point, although death appears to be far from Achaian thoughts during this typical scene of *thysia*.

As noted, the commensality theory of Vernant and Detienne might be presumed to apply, although the horizontal commensality among mortals is weighted more heavily than the vertical (mortal and immortal), as most of this scene concerns the preparing of meat. The tribute to the god is limited to eight out of twenty-one verses (1:447–468). Two of those are formal addresses describing the god (1:451–453); Chryses' prayer constitutes four more (1:453–456), and another three describe the preparing and burning of the god's portion (1:461–463). If there is any fallenness (Prometheus style) felt to this sacrifice, it is unstated, although clearly a respectful gulf is presumed between the Achaians and Apollo. Because the scene is quite precise and does not reach narratively beyond the immediate context, it is difficult to see how this relates to a structuralist map of Classical semiotic codes. Perhaps surprisingly, it is Tylor's theory, wherein sacrifice can be understood to propitiate spirits, that can be understood as most applicable here. Presumably that is because his theory is so simple.

Horkia: *Oath-Sacrificing Rituals*

Before describing the *Iliad*'s *horkia* rituals, distinctions among Homeric *horkos*, *horkia pista*, and *horkia* should be explained. *Horkos*, as opposed to *horkia*, has a few different meanings in Liddell and Scott's *Greek-English Lexicon*, the most obvious of which is oath. *Horkos* is used five times in the *Iliad*. We see it in Achilles' oath by the scepter at 1:233. We see it in Hera's oath not to have deceived Zeus at 15:37–38 and in the oath she coaxed Zeus into swearing in order to foil Heracles in the story at 19:109. We see it in the oath Odysseus coaxes Agamemnon to swear in order to reconcile with Achilles at 19:172 and in the oath Hector contemplates swearing to Achilles in exchange for his life at 22:119. None of these involve animal sacrifices.

Horkia pista, however, is used just as frequently, often in conjunction with *tamnō*, to cut, and it is used primarily in reference to oath-rituals. *Horkia pista* is used when Paris invites the Achaians and Trojans to cut oaths of friendship in 3:73; when Agamemnon muses about cutting oaths for the purpose of census at 2:124; when preparations for oath-sacrifice are made at

3:252; in the actual oath-sacrifice at 3:269; when Agamemnon laments over
the wound of Menelaos at 4:157 that the oaths he cut with the Trojans were
worthless; and when Achilles rejects Hector's appeal for an oath to return
the loser's body to his family at 22:266. *Horkia* alone is used at 2:339, when
Nestor complains that the Achaians have forgotten their oaths; at 4:236
when Agamemnon declares that Zeus will punish oath-violators; at 4:270
when Trojan Idomeneus seemingly agrees with Agamemnon that the
Trojans should be punished as oath-violators; and at 7:69 when Hector
reaffirms the terms of the oath from Book 3 in his duel with Ajax. The
practice is inferred by other vocabulary as well, such as the verb *omnumi*, to
swear, *euchomai*, to pray, or *epiorkon*, for a false oath, as well as by gestures,
such as Zeus nodding to a promise at 1:503–530. (See appendix in Kitts
2005/2011.) Because of the use of *horkia* in the context of sacrifices, it is the
term of preference here.

In terms of narrative power, *horkia* scenes are more ritually weighty than
thysia scenes with their bustling activity and ultimate satiation. *Horkia*
scenes instead are poetically somber, as expressed by their ponderous
rhythm and lethal phrasing, which culminate in the killing of a victim and
in imprecations against oath-violators. There are only two full *horkia* killing
scenes in the *Iliad*, in Books 3 and 19, but, similarly to *thysia* scenes, they are
tightly patterned, with six identical or quasi-identical phrases and many of
the eleven steps mirroring each other. Whereas *thysia* scenes indicate a busy
series of micro-actions, with twenty-five finite verbs in only fifteen verses
(not counting the prayers), *horkia* scenes feature slightly more than one
indicative verb per every two verses – precisely fourteen indicative verbs in
twenty-four verses (this too is discounting the prayers) – so the pace is far
slower and heavier. There is an unrelenting mood of menace.

Using the longer ritual in Book 3 as our model, we see that, first, there is
a sudden halt in battle, a clustering of weapons from both sides (3:113–115),
and both the Trojans and Achaians sit quietly (3:77–83; as too at 19:255–
256) on the ground to witness the oath. Then oath-victims (*horkia pista*) are
presented and the hands of the king are washed (3:268–270); King
Agamemnon draws his sacrificial knife ("his *machaira*, which always hung
by the sheath of his sword" [3:271–272; identical at 19:252–253]); he cuts
hairs from two lambs held by heralds, who distribute the hairs to the others

(3:273–274); holding up his hands, he prays (3:275, slight word variation at 19:254); he invokes Zeus, Earth, Helios, and the Erinyes (3:276–378, quasi-identical at 19:256–257) "who punish men, whosoever should swear a false oath" (3:279, identical at 19:260); he compels them: "you be witnesses, and protect the sworn oaths" (3:280); he provides the content of the oath (3:281–291; 19:261–263); then he "cut" (*tame*) the throat of the victim(s) "with the pitiless bronze" (3:292; quasi-identical at 19:266, with the boar substituted for the lambs). In Book 3 he puts the lambs on the ground "gasping, deprived of life and strength by the bronze" (3:293–294).[57] The participants then pour libations and pray; each of them would say (*eipesken* – the verb is distributive) may the brains of perjurers and their children run to the ground as does the wine, while their wives are subdued by others (3:298–301).

Another somber difference from *thysia* rituals is that the drawing of the *machaira* – a knife never even mentioned in *thysia* – is awarded two ominous verses – "Atreides, drawing with his hands the *machaira*/ which always hung by the great sheath of his sword" – and its killing work is inexorable: hence the epithet "the pitiless bronze" when he actually cuts the throat of the victim(s) (3:292, 19:266). Rather than the culinary verb *sphazdō* to denote slaughter, the verb for killing is *tamnō*, a concrete verb that here refers to cutting, specifically cutting the throat; the lambs gasp out their lives.[58] In *thysia* the gods get a nod in the form of a proffered libation and a fatty offering, whereas in *horkia* they are invoked to sanction the oath's violation with the most dreadful of punishments, illustrated by the mutilation of the animal victim and the analogy of brains when the participants pour wine.

In sum, *thysia* and *horkia* scenes have very little in common, which should make us question the modern umbrella term of "sacrifice" for the two Homeric scenes altogether. First, the *thysia* scene is lively with

---

[57] Whereas in Book 19 the herald hurls the boar into the river to become food for fish (19.267–268).

[58] "Cutting oaths" is a frequent expression used for oath-making across the Mediterranean world, although what is cut is disputed. See Bickerman (1976) and Weinfeld (1990).

preparations for and joy in a feast, whereas the *horkia* scene in Book 3 is quiet and serious, and its beginning is freighted with foreboding. Second, whereas the killing of *thysia*'s victims is masked by the verb for slaughter (*sphazdō*) and by butchering details (flaying, skewering, roasting), the killing is really the core of the oath-ritual, meant to be analogous to punishment for those who violate oaths.

Let us again try to find some kind of correlation between what happens here and the theories summarized earlier. Tylor's theories about "spiritual beings" who are reached by gifts would be hard to dismiss, as these rituals do strive to solicit a divine response: the gods are asked to witness and fulfill the oaths. Frazer's notion of homeopathic or mimetic magic might also seem to apply, as the ritual gesture of killing animal victims is expected to effect the deaths of human victims, at least in the imaginations of those taking part in the ritual. However, taking these oath-rituals on their faces – and the killing scenes are very graphic – these theories seemingly lack the muscle to capture the sinister intent of oath-making rituals. That intent is to bring suffering and death to anyone who might dare to violate the terms of the oath. Giving Frazer a bit of credit for his homeopathic approach, we nonetheless need to reach beyond these nineteenth-century theories to ritual theories (see the next section) if we want to capture the deadly effects.

The totemic theories of Freud, Robertson Smith, and Durkheim might have limited applicability here, as the gaze of the witnesses (and the poet) is clearly on the animal and his death is expected to be witnessed too by the gods. Insofar as Robertson Smith's and Durkheim's theories address a felt connection among the animals, gods, and sacrificers, the close focalization on the animals, especially on the two lambs in Book 3, might support the connection, particularly as gods and humans both are invited to witness the killing. No totemic relationship with the animals is established beforehand, however, which would seem to diminish the power of the totemic theories to explain oath-sacrifice since those theories posit a preexisting kinship. As for Freud, there is obviously no patricidal trauma that can be felt, presuming we are taking the ritual on its face.

Jonathan Z. Smith's gnostic theory would only fit if we were to presume a contemporary perspective, that no one could possibly believe that oath-rituals call upon gods to inflict punishments on oath-violators. As we typically suspend disbelief in giving ourselves over to reading ancient literatures and ritual narratives, to analyze this ancient oral poem from his skeptical perspective would not seem to take us very far toward understanding what the rituals were expected to mean for ancient audiences. We will revisit what they were expected to mean in Section 4.

Vernant and Detienne's theory of commensal sacrifice obviously will have very limited applicability, as they do not attempt to explain this more lethal kind of sacrifice but strictly the culinary one. The lateral bonding effects of ritual sacrifice might be presumed relevant – the participants sit quietly in Books 3 and 19 to witness the ritual, and they pile their weapons in the center in Book 3 – but they do not dine on the animal and it would be a stretch to incorporate later commensal mythologies into this very early poetic representation of oath-sacrifice. Homeric oath-sacrifices would appear to fall outside of their structuralist map of semiotic codes.

Nancy Jay's theory of patrilineal descent being manufactured through ritual sacrifice is only relevant here by a stretch, as no apparent expiation and communion are taking place and the exclusively male identities of the participants are taken for granted. The cursing threat goes so far as to portend harm to their wives and children, which suggests a relationship of concern, not abandonment of women, nor is there an apparent transcendence of mortality via male bonding. As with the other theories, this one reaches too far beyond the evidence to fit the Homeric *horkia* scene; it asks us to read far behind the Homeric verses.

As for Bataille and the sense of immanence for those undertaking the killing or witnessing, his theory seems most apt for this scene, if in fact the theory is not thoroughly romanticized. The focalization on the victims is clearly the point of Book 3's sacrifice, although it is unclear if the witnesses' attentions are more captivated by the killing or by the lethal punishments promised in the accompanying imprecation, which they intone collectively: "Zeus greatest and best and all the other immortal gods, whoever is first to violate the oaths, so may their brains run to the ground as does this wine, as well as those of their children, and may their wives be overpowered by others"

(3:298–301).[59] According to Bataille the killing of the animal exerts its own power on witnesses, although there is some ambiguity about the animal's status as a thing: "The individual identifies with the victim in the sudden movement that restores it to immanence (to intimacy), but the assimilation that is linked to the return to immanence is nonetheless based on the fact that the victim is the thing, just as the sacrificer is the individual" (2011:51). Thus, for Bataille, sacrifice is both destructive of the thing and transformative in inducing one's sense of immanence with the victim destroyed. His theory might indeed apply to the ritual killings in the *Iliad*, but primarily insofar as we relate to the gasping of the lambs as they die (human parallels touched upon in Section 1). This would seem to be an artistic consideration based upon a figurative understanding of dying animals as dying humans for the audience to the poem (as discussed in the references to Ricoeur). But as pointed out earlier about Bataille's lack of anthropology or ethnography, how far beyond poetic representation can Bataille's artistic account reach?

If there is any fascination with religious violence per se, as in a shiver of awe at ritual killing, as argued by Burkert, Girard, Freud, Jensen, it is surely restricted to oath-rituals in the *Iliad*. The lethal dimensions are obvious not only in the staged killing of the oath-victims but also in the spoken curse for similar punishments to be extended to oath-violators. There does seem to be a fascination with violence, but can it be grasped fully as a collective end product of mimetic rivalry (Girard), a dema legacy and resulting *Egriffenheit* (Jensen), an Oedipal trauma (Freud), or a legacy of the hunter's bipolar emotions at the spectacle of the kill (Burkert)? Any of these might be argued to apply but, leaning on Occam's razor and examining the ritual narrative on its face, these four theories each attempt to explain too much. The lethal threat is apparent to anyone with a body: need we reach beyond that into obscure sociologies, mythologies, and paleolithic legacies?

---

[59] Autenreith: "work mischief by violating the oaths" (www.perseus.tufts.edu /hopper/morph?l=phmh%2Fneian%26la=greek%26can=phmh%2Fneian0% 26prior=o(/rkia%26d=Perseus:text:1999.01.0133:book=3:card=264% 26i=1#lexicon).

Ultimately the ancient Near Eastern world itself provides analogs for the kind of staged cruelty we see in the *Iliad* and for the power of curses in oath-texts.[60] Exploring those should allow us to evaluate the Homeric sacrifice in its proper Near Eastern context, as well as to enlist some theories of ritual dynamics. These can be shown as better tools for analyzing the oath-rituals than can the grand sacrificial theories.

4 Ritual Dynamics and Ancient Near Eastern Cursing Texts

In its threatening dimension, the Homeric oath-ritual is not unique for the world of the ancient Near East, as evident in the abundance of cursing texts. Cursing texts are found in diplomatic correspondence extending from Mesopotamia west to Greece and dated over the last three millennia BCE. Curses conclude treaties and they are reported in correspondence about treaties. Their violations are invoked as causal in royal reports of military conquest, especially in Assyria. As does the Homeric oath-ritual, these cursing texts feature a threat of corporeal injury extending often beyond individual oath-violators to their families should an oath be violated. As does the Homeric ritual, this threat is analogized to the pain and suffering of the animal victim. Consider these neo-Assyrian examples:

> This shoulder is not the shoulder of a spring lamb, it is the shoulder of Mati'ilu, it is the shoulder of his sons, his magnates, and the people of his land. If Mati'ilu should sin against this treaty, so may, just as the shoulder of this spring lamb is torn out . . . the shoulder of Mati'ilu, of his sons, [his magnates] and the people of his land be torn out.
>
> (Arnold and Beyer 2002:101)

> [J]ust as [thi]s ewe has been cut open and the flesh of [her] young has been placed in her mouth, may they make you eat

---

[60] Parallels between Hittite and Homeric feasting scenes have been explored elsewhere (e.g., Kitts 2011).

in your hunger the flesh of your brothers, your sons and
your daughters.   (Luckenbill 1968[1926]:52, section 69)

Just as young sheep and ewes and male and female spring
lambs are slit open and their entrails rolled down over their
feet, so may (your entrails and) the entrails of your sons and
your daughters roll down over your feet.
                         (Parpola and Watanabe 1988, section 70)

Since texts are our primary evidence for these, we cannot be certain
whether these texts describe actual mutilations of animals or just scribal
imaginations of such mutilations, but their menacing intentions cannot be
disputed. Notice that, while explicit cosmic agents may be invoked to effect
punishments, as in the *Iliad*, in many cases the agent is only inferred,
apparently less significant to the scribes than the vivid description of
corporeal abuse. The ancient Near Eastern artistic repertoire outside of
cursing texts is already rich with meaningful renderings of mutilated bodies
(Bahrani 2008; Dolce 2017). This could make it questionable whether our
response to such spectacles, or the imagination of them, is quite comparable
to that of ancient audiences, who might well be inured to spectacles such as
these. Nonetheless it is also true that the intent of these curses is precisely to
trigger a response – why else would they be so graphic? Here, using lessons
from sensory anthropology we can show, tentatively and in brief, how
rituals that display corporeal abuse not only enact force on ritual victims but
also communicate its effects to witnesses. This argument involves understanding the apperception of pain, ritual communication, and engaged
seeing – all three relatively new rubrics for the anthropological study of
ritualized violence.

Ritually Induced Pain

The study of ritually induced pain is part of a wave of sensory anthropology
that strives to grasp experiences that often elude language. Since Elaine
Scarry (1994[1985]), pain has been argued to engage us at a level deeper
than discourse and potentially to precipitate transformations in perceived

realities (see too Morinis 1985; Beidelman 1997; Glucklich 2003), even to confer a quality of "incontestable reality" on the force deemed to have brought pain into being (e.g., spirits, ancestors, oath-gods). Once seared into consciousness, it is said, pain can become a powerful mnemonic device for creating context and anchoring signification (Rappaport 1999:147), as we see too in ritual ordeals initiating engagement in warrior bands and in other high-intensity group dynamics (Whitehouse 2004:105–118; Alcorta and Sosis 2005).

The focus on the transformative dimensions of pain is of obvious relevance to the voiceless oath-victims, but what about to the witnesses? Based on the theories of ritual communication and art sketched in what follows, it can be argued that the specter of physical pain can conjure in witnesses sensations they intuit by engaged seeing. In oath-rituals, spectacles of suffering are meant to educe witnesses to introject the victim's pain into themselves and to become aware of potential punishments due those on the wrong side of the oath.

Ritual Communication

To grasp how this works, first we must understand how ritual communicates. One of the pioneers of the theory of ritual communication was Stanley Tambiah, who described the meaning communicated by ritual as a matter of pattern recognition and figural awareness (1979:134). Successful ritual spectacles communicate with audiences who grasp familiar iconic shapes through the prism of an emergent performance. "Emergent meanings [riding] on the already existing grids of symbolic and indexical meanings, while also displaying new resonances" is one way he put it (160, cf. 119). Simply, these performances effectively communicate when audiences recognize the underlying tradition emergent in a new instantiation. In this case the tradition is oath-making.

But the rituals just described are extraordinary in that they do not simply communicate a familiar pattern of swearing an oath, but do so in an elevated performance register.[61] These are not simple killings, as in culinary rituals, but meaning-laden performances that convey unmistakable menace,

---

[61] For a summary of the notion, see Kitts (2018a:58–70).

a feature far outside most of the sacrificial theories discussed earlier. The significance is deadly: betraying the terms of the oath invites a corporeal threat. To grasp this menacing dimension, we need to understand further the dynamics of engaged seeing for which the studies of artistic and ritual spectacles coincide.

Engaged Seeing

Since Susanne Langer we have been told that certain artworks engage the eye organically through the presentation of rhythms, tensions, and resolutions that we perceive through repetitions and variations of shapes, colors, and textures (1951:217–224; 1953:373–374). Our intuition of these is reportedly nondiscursive and similar to the way we experience sound (Howes 2011); sound elicits a visceral response in our bodies, as does seeing before we label and explain it, when we are first drawn to what we see. David Morgan describes the haptic dimension of seeing. He points out that, in seeing, we may introject onto ourselves sensory features of the seen, such as texture, touch, movement (2012:111–126), and presumably too susceptibility to the experience of pain. In 2018 he followed Roland Barthes in noting the ability of some images to "prick" the viewer, wherein what we see gets enfolded in the "robust domain of embodiment, feeling, and thought" (Morgan 2018:48). Both the haptic dimension of seeing and the pricking effect are conceivable for an audience responding to the spectacle of tortured oath-victims. Indeed the ritual tradition relies on these effects to communicate its intent.

Morgan also points out the influence of mood on seeing. Moods can "conduct the visual construction of reality" (Morgan 2012:22–25, 33) whereby particular elements stand out to us and stand against each other in a notable array. Goran Aijmer approaches this from the perspective of iconic communication, noting how "symbolic displays of strong expressive force, . . . working outside language . . . and thus without referential meaning" can be instrumental in envisioning, building, and altering possible worlds (2000:3), and presumably too in threatening them. These effects are all the more powerful because they elude discourse and yet are felt. It is easy to imagine that the oath-ritual of *Iliad* Book 3, given the silence and stilling of battle that precede it and the utter seriousness with which it is conducted, corresponds to this account of mood, which helps conduct the visual construction of a very lethal reality. In terms of iconic communication, the specialized ritual personae and instruments – for example, the heralds and the king's *machaira* – help elevate the register of the occasion. The ritual in *Iliad* Book 3 is a familiar but deadly event, as must have been the rituals behind the Assyrian curses mentioned earlier.

Last, Tobin Siebers studied the effects of trauma art wherein representations of torture and maiming reputedly precipitate startling awarenesses of our corporeal frailty in the face of force (2003). According to his theory, trauma art offers canvases for contemplating the kind of meanings we once pondered through religious rituals and stories – through martyrologies, for instance, which may detail the effects of force on bodies (see Collins 1994; Grig 2002; Cobb 2017). Although Siebers' theory addresses the postmodern saturation with violent spectacles, historians of ancient art will attest that this fascination with trauma art is not unique to our era. The plenum of graphic suffering in ancient art and prose has been noted by Dolce (2017) and Bahrani (2008), among others. However historically contingent our understandings of pain, these oath-making spectacles are plausible instances wherein the specter of animal wounding and death is expected to "transubstantiate," as Siebers calls it (2003:15), the victims' fear and pain into witnesses. The whole premise of the oath-killing rituals is that we do transubstantiate this pain. In this menacing dimension these are not generically different from certain terroristic threat videos that we find today (Kitts 2020). From this brief account of the dynamics of ancient cursing rituals, we can see that ritual, artistic, and sensory theories offer a more cogent picture of the dynamics of oath-sacrifices than do the universalizing sacrificial theories discussed in Section 3.

Conclusion

This short Element has offered an overview of themes, theories, and controversies relating to the scholarly study of sacrifice. It began with two sensational topics that have become impossible to extricate from the study of sacrifice, namely patriotic death as sacrifice and literary reports of premodern human ritual killings. The first is reputedly rooted in the early Western war epic, the *Iliad*, but is in fact well developed in later literature and popular understanding all the way into our own time. The second is vastly attested in rumor, but three well-researched cultures where the practice is supported by literary evidence are the ancient Aztec, Chinese, and Classical Greek cultures. Section 1 comprised descriptions of these themes. Section 2 summarized theories of sacrifice, beginning with a few embryonic theories in biblical, Vedic, and Greek texts, and then focusing on theories from the nineteenth and twentieth centuries, from Tylor through Girard, Burkert, Smith, Vernant and Detienne, J. Z. Smith, Jay, Bataille, and de Hesuch. Section 3 reviewed the *Iliad*'s commensal (*thysia*) and oath (*horkia*) sacrifices. It described them as the products of oral traditional composition and then attempted to gauge how far our universalizing theories of the nineteenth and twentieth centuries could be stretched to explain them. Not very far, it turns out, which is one reason these universalizing theories are rejected for analyzing ancient sacrifices. It turns out that the Homeric *thysia* and *horkia* scenes differ radically in their moods, features, and ascertainable purposes, which is why the term "sacrifice" for these rituals is ill fitting and arguably anachronistic. This brings us to an alternative hypothesis. Section 4 attempts to appreciate Homeric oath-sacrifices and cursing rituals in ancient Near Eastern context and from the perspective of ritual theory rather than sacrificial theory. Sensory anthropology is found to be a better fit than sacrificial theory for grasping the menacing nature of oath-sacrifices in the ancient Near East.

References

Aijmer, Göran. 2000. "Introduction: The Idiom of Violence in Imagery and Discourse." In *Meanings of Violence: A Cross-Cultural Perspective*. Edited by Jon Abbink and Göran Aijmer. Berg. 1–54.

Alcorta, Candace, and Richard Sosis. 2005. "Ritual, Emotion, and Sacred Symbols." *Human Nature* 16(4):323–359.

Arnold, Bill, and Bryan Beyer. 2002. *Readings from the Ancient Near East*. Baker Academic.

Autenrieth, George. 1958. *A Homeric Dictionary*. Translated by Robert P. Keep. Revised by Isaac Flagg. University of Oklahoma Press.

Bahrani, Zeinab. 2008. *Rituals of War*. Zone Books.

Bakker, Egbert, and Florence Fabbricotti. 1991. "Peripheral and Nuclear Semantics in Homeric Diction." *Mnemosyne* 44:63–84.

Barton, Carlin A. 1994. "Savage Miracles: The Redemption of Lost Honor in Roman Society and the Sacrament of the Gladiator and the Martyr." *Representations* 45:41–71.

2002. "Honor and Sacredness in the Roman and Christian Worlds." In *Sacrificing the Self: Perspectives on Martyrdom and Religion*. Edited by Margaret Cormack. Oxford University Press. 23–38.

Bataille, Georges. 2011. *Theory of Religion*. Translated by Hurley. Zone Books.

Bateson, Gregory. 1972. *Steps to an Ecology of Mind*. Ballentine Books.

Beidelman, Thomas O. 1997. *The Cool Knife: Imagery of Gender, Sexuality, and Moral Education in Kaguru Initiation Ritual*. Smithsonian Institution Press.

Bellah, Robert N. 2005. "Civil Religion in America." *Daedalus* 134 (4):40–55. www.jstor.org/stable/20028013

Benn, James A. 2007. *Burning for the Buddha: Self-Immolation in Chinese Buddhism*. University of Hawaii Press.

Bickerman, Daniel R. 1976. "Couper une alliance." *Studies in Jewish and Christian History*, Vol. 1. Brill. 1–32.

Bloch, Maurice. 1989. *Ritual, History and Power: Selected Papers in Anthropology*. Berg.

Bonnechere, Pierre. 2013. *Le sacrifice humain dans la pensée grecque*. Presses universitaires de Liége. Kernos suppléments. https://books .openedition.org/pulg/1041

Bremmer, Jan N. 1983. "Scapegoat Rituals in Ancient Greece." *Harvard Studies in Classical Philology* 87:299–320.

  2007. "Myth and Ritual in Greek Human Sacrifice: Lykaon, Polyxena, and the Case of the Rhodian Criminal." In *The Strange World of Human Sacrifice*. Edited by Bremmer. Peeters. 55–77.

Bryce, Trevor. 2006. *The Trojans and Their Neighbors*. Routledge.

Burkert, Walter. 1983. *Homo Necans*. University of California Press.

  1987. "The Problem of Ritual Killing." In *Violent Origins: Ritual Killing and Cultural Formation*. Edited by Robert G. Hamerton-Kelly. Stanford University Press. 149–190.

  1996. *Creation of the Sacred: Tracks of Biology in Early Religions*. Harvard University Press.

  2013. "Sacrificial Violence: A Problem in Ancient Religions." In *Oxford Handbook of Religion and Violence*. Edited by Mark Juergensmeyer, Margo Kitts, and Michael Jerryson. Oxford University Press. 437–453.

Cairns, Douglas L. 2001. "Introduction." In *Oxford Readings in Homer's Iliad*. Edited by Douglas L. Cairns. Oxford University Press. 1–56.

  2003. "Ethics, Ethology, Terminology: Iliadic Anger and the Cross-Cultural Study of Emotion." In *Ancient Anger, Perspectives from Homer to Galen*. Edited by Susanna Braund and Glenn W. Most. Cambridge University Press. 11–50.

Carrasco, David. 1999. *City of Sacrifice*. Beacon Press.

2013. "Sacrifice/Human Sacrifice in Religious Traditions." In *Oxford Handbook of Religion and Violence*. Edited by Mark Juergensmeyer, Margo Kitts, and Michael Jerryson. Oxford University Press. 208–225.

Cobb, L. Stephanie. 2008. *Dying to Be Men: Gender and Language in Early Christian Martyr Texts*. Columbia University Press.

2017. *Divine Deliverance: Pain and Painlessness in Early Christian Martyr Texts*. University of California Press. https://doi.org/10.1525/california/9780520293359.001.0001

Collins, Adela Yarbro. 1994. "From Noble Death to Crucified Messiah." *New Testament Studies* 40:491–503.

Connelly, Joan Benton. 2007. *Portrait of a Priestess: Women and Ritual in Ancient Greece*. Princeton University Press.

Considine, Patrick. 1969. "The Theme of Divine Wrath in Ancient East Mediterranean Literature." *Studi Micenei ed Egeo-Anatolici* 8:85–159.

Daly, Robert J. 2003(1990). "The Power of Sacrifice in Ancient Judaism and Christianity." In *Understanding Religious Sacrifice: A Reader*. Edited by Jeffrey Carter. Bloomsbury. 342–356.

2009. *Sacrifice Unveiled: The True Meaning of Christian Sacrifice*. Bloomsbury.

de Heusch, Luc. 1985. *Sacrifice in Africa*. Indiana University Press.

Detienne, Marcel. 1994. *The Gardens of Adonis*. Princeton University Press.

Detienne, Marcel, and Jean-Pierre Vernant. 1978. *Cunning Intelligence in Greek Culture and Society*. Translated by Janet Lloyd. Harvester Press Limited.

1989. *The Cuisine of Sacrifice among the Greeks*. University of Chicago Press.

Dolce, Rita. 2017. *Losing One's Head in the Ancient Near East: Interpretation and Meaning of Decapitation*. Routledge.

Droge, Arthur J., and James D. Tabor. 1992. *A Noble Death: Suicide and Martyrdom among Christians and Jews in Antiquity*. Harper San Francisco.

Durkheim, Emile. 2001. *Elementary Forms of Religious Life*. Translated by Carol Cosman. Oxford University Press.

Eberhart, Christian. 2011. *Ritual and Metaphor: Sacrifice in the Bible*. Society of Biblical Literature. https://hdl.handle.net/2027/heb.31351

Evans-Pritchard, Edward Evan. 1965. *Theories of Primitive Religion*. Clarendon.

Faraone, Christopher. 2019. "Animal-Effigies in Ancient Curses: The Role of Gender, Age and Natural Behavior in Their Selection." *Mediterraneo Antico* 22(1–2): 307–334.

Fenech, Louis E. 2018. "The Tropics of Heroic Death: Martyrdom and the Sikh Tradition." In *Martyrdom, Self-Sacrifice, and Self-Immolation: Religious Perspectives on Suicide*. Edited by Margo Kitts. Oxford University Press. 205–225.

Ferguson, R. Brian. 2006. "Archaeology, Cultural Anthropology, and the Origins and Intensifications of War." In *Archaeology of Warfare: Prehistories of Raiding and Conquest*. Edited by Elizabeth N. Arkush and Mark W. Allen. University of Florida Press. 469–523.

Fernandez, James W. 1977. "The Performance of Ritual Metaphors." In *Social Use of Metaphor*. Edited by J. David Sapir and J. Christopher Crocker. University of Pennsylvania Press. 100–131.

Frazer, James George. 1951. *The Golden Bough: A Study in Magic and Religion*, Vol. 1, abridged. MacMillan.

Frisk, Hjalmar. 1946. "ΜΗΝΙΣ: Zur Geschichte eines Begriffes." *Eranos* 44:28–40.

Freud, Sigmund. 1946(1918). *Totem and Taboo*. Translated by A. A. Brills. Vintage Books.

1961(1927). *Future of an Illusion*. Translated by Strachey. W. W. Norton and Company. https://archive.org/stream/sigmund-freud-the-future -of-an-illusion/sigmund-freud-the-future-of-an-illusion_djvu.txt

Gaposchkin, M. Cecilia. 2017. *Invisible Weapons*. Princeton University Press.

Geertz, Clifford. 2000(1983). *Local Knowledge: Further Essays in Interpretive Anthropology*. Basic Books.

Gilders, William K. n.d. "Sacrifice in Ancient Israel." www.bibleodyssey .org/en/passages/related-articles/sacrifice-in-ancient-israel

Girard, René. 1977. *Violence and the Sacred*. Translated by Patrick Gregory. Johns Hopkins University Press.

1987. *Things Hidden since the Foundation of the World*. Translated by Stephen Bann and Michael Metteer. Stanford University Press.

1996. *The Girard Reader*. Edited by James O. Williams. Crossroads.

2011. *Breakthroughs in Mimetic Theory: Sacrifice*. Translated by Matthew Pattillo and David Dawson. Michigan State University Press.

2014a. *Studies in Violence, Mimesis, and Culture: One by Whom Scandal Comes*. Translated by M. B. DeBevoise. Michigan State University Press.

2014b. *Studies in Violence, Mimesis, and Culture: When These Things Begin: Conversations with Michel Treguer*. Translated by Trevor Cribben Merrill. Michigan State University Press.

Glucklich, Ariel. 2003. *Sacred Pain*. Oxford University Press.

Gorski, Philip. 2017. *American Covenant: A History of Civil Religion from the Puritans to the Present*. Princeton University Press.

Graziano, Frank. 2006(1999). *The Millennial New World*. Oxford University Press. https://doi.org/10.1093/0195124324.001.0001

Griffiths, Alan H. 2016. "Tantalus." *Oxford Classical Dictionary Online*. https://doi.org/10.1093/acrefore/9780199381135.013.6218

Grig, Lucy. 2002. "Torture and Truth in Late Antique Martyrology." *Early Medieval Europe* 2(4): 321–336.

Grottanelli, Cristiano. 1988. "Uccidere, donare, mangiare." In *Sacrificio e societá nel mondo antico*. Edited by Cristiano Grottanelli and Nicola F. Parese. Laterza. 3–53.

Haider, Najam. 2018. "The Death of Mūsā al-Kāzim (d.183/799): Knowledge and Suicide in Early Twelver Shīʿism." In *Martyrdom, Self-Sacrifice, and Self-Immolation: Religious Perspectives on Suicide*. Edited by Margo Kitts. Oxford University Press. 106–125.

Hamerton-Kelly, Robertson G., editor. 1987. *Violent Origins. Walter Burkert, René Girard, and Jonathan Z. Smith on Ritual Killing and Cultural Formation*. Stanford University Press.

Hengel, Martin. 1977. *Crucifixion in the Ancient World and the Folly of the Message of the Cross*. Translated by John Bowden. Fortress Press.

    1981. *Atonement: The Origins of the Doctrine in the New Testament*. Fortress Press.

Henrichs, Albert. 2000. "Drama and Dromena: Bloodshed, Violence, and Sacrificial Metaphor in Euripides." *Harvard Studies in Classical Philology* 100:173–188.

Heesterman, Johannes C. 1984. "Non-violence and Sacrifice." *Indologica Taurinensia* 12:119–127.

    1993. *The Broken World of Sacrifice: An Essay in Ancient Indian Ritual*. University of Chicago Press.

Howes, David. 2011. "Sensation." *Material Religion* 7(1):92–98. https://doi.org/10.2752/175183411X12968355482178

Hubert, Henri, and Marcel Mauss. 1968. *Sacrifice: Its Nature and Function*. University of Chicago Press.

Huffman, Carl. 2015. "Pythagoras." *The Stanford Encyclopedia of Philosophy* (Winter 2018 Edition). Edited by Edward N. Zalta. https://plato.stanford.edu/archives/win2018/entries/pythagoras

Hughes, Dennis D. 1991. *Human Sacrifice in Ancient Greece*. Routledge.

Insoll, Timothy. 2012. "Sacrifice." In *The Oxford Handbook of the Archaeology of Ritual and Religion*. Edited by Timothy Insoll. Oxford University Press. https://doi.org/10.1093/oxfordhb/9780199232444.013.0063

Janko, Richard. 1992. *The Iliad: A Commentary. Vol. IV: Books 13–16*. Cambridge University Press.

Janzen, David. 2020. "Sin and Expiation." In *The Oxford Handbook of Ritual and Worship in the Hebrew Bible*. Edited by Samuel E. Balentine. Oxford University Press. 1–14. https://doi.org/10.1093/oxfordhb/9780190222116.013.17

Jay, Nancy. 1992. *Throughout Your Generations Forever: Sacrifice, Religion, and Paternity*. University of Chicago Press.

Jensen, Adolf E. 1963(1951). *Myth and Cult among Primitive Peoples*. Translated by Marianna Tax Choldin and Wolfgang Weissleder. University of Chicago Press.

Juergensmeyer, Mark, and Margo Kitts, editors. 2011. *Princeton Readings in Religion and Violence*. Princeton University Press.

Katz, Marilyn A. 1992. "Ox-Slaughter and Goring Oxen: Homicide, Animal Sacrifice, and Judicial Process." *Yale Journal of Law and the Humanities* 4 (2)(3). 249–278http://digitalcommons.law.yale.edu/yjlh/vol4/iss2/3

Kitts, Margo. 2002. "Sacrificial Violence in the *Iliad*." *Journal of Ritual Studies* 16:19–39.

2005. *Sanctified Violence in Homeric Society*. Cambridge University Press.

2008. "Funeral Sacrifices and Ritual Leitmotifs in *Iliad* 23." In *Transformations in Sacrificial* Practices, *Performanzen* Band *15*. Edited by E. Stavrianopoulou et al. LIT-Verlag. 217–240.

2010. "*Poinē* As a Ritual Leitmotif in the *Iliad*." *State, Power and Violence*. Vol. 3 of *Ritual Dynamics and the Science of Ritual*. Edited by Margo Kitts, et al. General editor Axel Michaels. Harrassowitz. 7–31.

2011. "Ritual Scenes in the *Iliad*." *Oral Tradition* 26(1):221–246.

2015. "Anthropology and the *Iliad*." In *Ashgate Research Companion to Anthropology*. Edited by Pamela Stewart and Andrew Strathern. Ashgate Press. 389–410.

2016. "Mimetic Theory, Sacrifice, and the *Iliad*?" *Bulletin of Religious Studies* 45(3).

2017. "Discursive, Iconic and Somatic Perspectives on Ritual." *Journal of Ritual Studies* 31(1):11–26.

2018a. *Elements of Ritual and Violence*. Cambridge University Press. www.cambridge.org/core/elements/elements-of-ritual-and violence /E4D15686F2A18B38E141EA16C9336BB5

2018b. "The *Martys* and Spectacular Death: From Homer to the Roman Arena." *Journal of Religion and Violence* 6(2):267–294. www .pdcnet.org/jrv/onlinefirst

2022. "Contemporary Perspectives on Religion and Violence." In *Encyclopedia of Violence, Peace, and Conflict*, Vol. 4. Edited by L. R. Kurtz. Elsevier Academic Press. 276–286. https://dx.doi.org /10.1016/B978-0-12-820195-4.00236-3.ISBN:9780128201954

Kitts, Margo, editor. 2018c. *Martyrdom, Self-Sacrifice, and Self-Immolation: Religious Perspectives on Suicide*. Oxford University Press. https:// global.oup.com/academic/product/martyrdom-self-sacrifice-and -self-immolation-9780190656485?cc=us&lang=en&

Klawans, Jonathan. 2001. "Pure Violence: Sacrifice and Defilement in Ancient Israel." *Harvard Theological Review* 94(2):133–155.

Kramer, Ross, editor. 2004. *Women's Religions in the Greco-Roman World: A Sourcebook*. Oxford University Press.

Langer, Susanne. 1951. *Philosophy in a New Key*. New American Library.
1953. *Feeling and Form: A Theory of Art*. MacMillan.

Lefkowitz, Mary R. 2007. *Women in Greek Myth*. Johns Hopkins University Press.

Levenson, Jon D. 1993. *The Death and Resurrection of the Beloved Son*. Yale University Press.
2013. *Inheriting Abraham*. Princeton University Press.

Liddell, Henry George, and Robert Scott. 1968. *A Greek-English Lexicon*. Clarendon.

Luckenbill, Daniel David. 1968(1926). *Ancient Records of Assyria and Babylonia*, Vol. 1. University of Chicago Press.

Mack, Burton. 1987. "Introduction: Religion and Ritual." In *Violent Origins: Ritual Killing and Cultural Formation*. Edited by Robert G. Hamerton-Kelly. Stanford University Press. 1–70.

March, Jenny. 2015. "Atreus." *Oxford Classical Dictionary Online*. https://doi.org/10.1093/acrefore/9780199381135.013.941

Marvin, Carolyn, and David W. Ingle. 1996. "Blood Sacrifice and the Nation: Revisiting Civil Religion." *Journal of the American Academy of Religion* 64(4):767–780.

Mauss, Marcel. 1973(1935). "Techniques of the Body." *Economy and Society* 2 (1):70–87. www.tandfonline.com/doi/abs/10.1080/03085147300000003

Mayor, Adrienne. 2015. "Warrior Women: The Myth and Reality of the Amazons." *Council on Foreign Relations*. May 6. www.foreignaffairs.com/articles/2015-06-05/adrienne-mayor-amazons

McCarty, Matthew M. 2019. "The Tophet and Infant Sacrifice." In *The Oxford Handbook of the Phoenician and Punic Mediterranean*. Edited by Carolina López-Ruiz and Brian Doak. https://doi.org/10.1093/oxfordhb/9780190499341.013.21

McClymond, Kathryn. 2002. "Death Be Not Proud: Reevaluating the Role of Killing in Sacrifice." *International Journal of Hindu Studies* 6(2):221–242.

2008. *Beyond Sacred Violence: A Comparative Study of Sacrifice*. John Hopkins University Press.

Milgrom, Jacob. 1998. *Leviticus 1–16*. Yale University Press.

Morgan, David. 2012. *The Embodied Eye*. University of California Press. 2018. *How Images Work*. Oxford University Press.

Morinis, Alan. 1985. "The Ritual Experience: Pain and the Transformation of Consciousness in Ordeals of Initiation." *Ethos* 13(2):150–174.

Moss, Candida R. 2010. *The Other Christs: Imitating Jesus in Ancient Christian Ideologies of Martyrdom*. Oxford Scholarship Online. https://doi.org/10.1093/acprof:oso/9780199739875.001.0001

Nagy, Gregory. 1990. *Greek Mythology and Poetics*. Cornell University Press.

Naiden, F. S. 2020. "Violent Sacrifice in the Ancient Greek and Roman Worlds." In *Cambridge World History of Violence: The Prehistoric and Ancient Worlds*. Edited by Garret G. Fagan, Linda Fibiger, Mark Hudson, and Matthew Trundle. Cambridge University Press. 475–492. https://doi.org/10.1017/9781316341247

Nasrallah, Laura. 2012. "The Embarrassment of Blood." In *Ancient Mediterranean Sacrifice*. Edited by Jennifer Wright Knust and Zsuzsanna Varhelyi. Oxford University Press. 1–35. https://doi.org/10.1093/acprof:oso/9780199738960.003.0007

Otto, Rudolf. 1958(1923). *The Idea of the Holy*. Translated by John W. Harvey. Oxford University Press.

Page, T. E., and W. H. D. Rouse, editors. 1961. *The Odes of Pindar, Including the Principal Fragments*. Loeb Classical Library.

Palaver, Wolfgang. 2021. *Transforming the Sacred into Saintliness*. Cambridge University Press.

Parpola, Asko. 2007. "Human Sacrifice in India in Vedic Times and Before." In *The Strange World of Human Sacrifice*. Edited by Bremmer. Peeters. 157–177.

Parpola, Simo, and Kazuko Watanabe, editors. 1988. *State Archives of Assyria, Vol II: Neo-Assyrian Treaties and Loyalty Oaths.* The Neo-Assyrian Text Corpus Project and the Helsinki Press.

Pirenne-Delforge, Vinciane. 2007. "'Something to do with Aphrodite': *Ta Aphrodisia* and the Sacred." In *A Companion to Greek Religion.* Edited by Daniel Ogden. Wiley. 311–322.

Pollock, Susan. 2007. "Death of a Household." In *Performing Death.* Edited by Nicola Laneri. University of Chicago. 209–222.

Pongratz-Leisten, Beate. 2007. "Ritual Killing and Sacrifice in the Ancient Near East." In *Human Sacrifice in Jewish and Christian Tradition.* Edited by Karin Finsterbusch, Armin Lange, and Diethard Römheld. Brill. 3–33.

    2012. "Sacrifice in the Ancient Near East: Offering and Ritual Killing." In *Sacred Killing: The Archaeology of Sacrifice in the Ancient Near East.* Edited by Anne Porter and Glenn M. Schwartz. Eisenbrauns. 291–304.

Rappaport, Roy A. 1999. *Ritual and Religion in the Making of Humanity.* Cambridge University Press.

Ricoeur, Paul. 1973. "The Model of the Text: Meaningful Action Considered As a Text." *New Literary History* 5(1):91–117.

    1981. "The Metaphorical Process As Cognition, Imagination, and Feeling." *Philosophical Perspectives on Metaphor.* Edited by Mark Johnson. University of Minnesota Press. 228–247. Reprinted from *Critical Inquiry* 5(1) (1978):143–159.

Robertson Smith, W. 1957(1988–1989). *The Religion of the Semites.* Meridian Books.

Ruane, N. J. 2013. *Sacrifice and Gender in Biblical Law.* Cambridge University Press.

Salimbetti, Andrea. 2021. "The Greek Age of Bronze: Body Shields." www.salimbeti.com/micenei/shields1.htm

Scarry, Elaine. 1994(1985). *The Body in Pain.* Oxford University Press.

Scheid, John. 2015. "Sacrifice, Roman." *Oxford Classical Dictionary*. https://doi.org/10.1093/acrefore/9780199381135.013.5657

Schonthal, Benjamin. 2018. "The Meanings of Sacrifice: The LTTE, Suicide, and the Limits of the Religion Question." In *Martyrdom, Self-Sacrifice, and Self-Immolation: Religious Perspectives on Suicide*. Edited by Margo Kitts. Oxford University Press. 226–240.

Schultz, Celia E. 2010. "The Romans and Ritual Murder." *Journal of the American Academy of Religion* 78(2):516–541. https://doi.org/10.1093/jaarel/lfq002

Schwartz, Glen M. 2012. "Archaeology and Sacrifice." In *Sacred Killing: The Archaeology of Sacrifice in the Ancient Near East*. Edited by Anne Porter and Glenn M. Schwartz. Eisenbrauns. 1–32.

Shaw, Brent D. 1996. "Body/Power/Identity: Passions of the Martyrs." *Journal of Early Christian Studies* 4(3):269–312. https://doi.org/10.1353/earl.1996.0037

Shelach, Gideon. 1996. "The Qiang and the Question of Human Sacrifice in the Late Shang Period." *Asian Perspectives* 35(1):1–26.

Shepkaru, Shmuel. 2002. "To Die for God: Martyrs' Heaven in Hebrew and Latin Crusade Narratives." *Speculum* 77(2):311–341.

Siebers, Tobin. 2003. "The Return to Ritual: Violence and Art in the Media Age." *Journal of Cultural and Religious Theory* 5(1):9–33.

Smith, Jonathan Z. 1973. "When the Bough Breaks." *History of Religions* 12 (4):342–371.

  1982. "Bare Facts of Ritual." In *Imagining Religion: From Babylon to Jonestown*. University of Chicago Press. 53–65.

  1987. "The Domestication of Sacrifice." In *Violent Origins: Ritual Killing and Cultural Formation*. Edited by Robert Hamerton-Kelly. Stanford University Press. 191–205.

  1990. *Drudgery Divine*. University of Chicago Press.

  2004. *Relating Religion*. University of Chicago Press.

Smith, Mark S. 2001/2003. "The Life and Death of Baal." In *The Origins of Biblical Monotheism: Israel's Polytheistic Background and the Ugaritic Texts*. Edited by Mark S. Smith. Oxford Scholarship Online. 1–56. https://doi.org/10.1093/019513480X.001.0001

Spencer, Herbert. 2003(1882). *The Principles of Sociology: Vol. I*. New York: D. Appleton and Company. Excerpted in Jeffrey Carter, ed. 2003. *Understanding Religious Sacrifice: A Reader*. Bloomsbury Publishing. 39–51.

Stromsa, Guy G. 2015. "The End of Sacrifice." In *The Making of the Abrahamic Religions in Late Antiquity*. Oxford Scholarship Online. https://doi.org/10.1093/acprof:oso/9780198738862.001.0001

Tambiah, Stanley J. 1979. "A Performative Approach to Ritual." In *Proceedings of the British Academy*, Vol. 65. Oxford University Press. 113–169.

Ter Haar, Barend. 2019. *Religious Culture and Violence in Traditional China*. Cambridge University Press.

Tse, Wicky. 2020. "Violence and Warfare in Early Imperial China." In *The Cambridge World History of Violence: The Prehistoric and Ancient Worlds*. Edited by Garret G. Fagan, Linda Fibiger, Mark Hudson, and Matthew Trundle. Cambridge University Press. 277–297.

Tylor, Edward Burnett. 1958. *Religion in Primitive Culture*, Vol. 2. Harper & Row.

    2003. "Edward Burnett Tylor (b. 1832)." In *Understanding Religious Sacrifice: A Reader*. Edited by Jeffrey Carter. Bloomsbury. 23–38.

Van Straten, F. T. 1995. *Hiera Kala: Images of Animal Sacrifice in Archaic and Classical Greece*. Brill.

Vasquez, Manuel A. 2011. *More than Belief: A Materialist Theory of Religion*. Oxford University Press.

Vernant, Pierre. 1978. "Introduction" to Detienne, *Gardens of Adonis: Spices in Greek Mythology*. Translated by Janet Lloyd. Princeton University Press.

1989. "At Man's Table: Hesiod's Foundation Myth of Sacrifice." In *The Cuisine of Sacrifice among the Greeks*. Edited by Marcel Detienne and Pierre Vernant. Translated by Paul Wissing. University of Chicago Press. 21–86.

Versnel, H. S. 2015. "Devotio." Oxford Classical Dictionary. Editor in Chief, Tim Whitmarsh. Oxford University Press. 1–2. https://doi.org/10.1093/acrefore/9780199381135.013.2134.

Visser, Edzard. 1988. "Formulae or Single Words? Towards a New Theory on Homeric Verse-Making." *Würzburger Jarbücher für die Altertumswissenchaft* 14:21–37.

Walsh, Thomas R. 2005. *Fighting Words and Feuding Words: Studies in the Semantics of Anger in Homeric Poetry*. Rowman and Littlefield.

Wang, Ping. 2008. "Methods of Killing Human Sacrifice in Shang-Dynasty Oracle-Bone Inscriptions." *minima sinica* 20(1):11–29.

Watts, James W. 2006. "'ōlāh: The Rhetoric of Burnt Offerings." *Vetus Testamentum* 56:1 (Jan. 2006):125–137.

2007. *Ritual and Rhetoric in Leviticus*. Cambridge University Press.

Weinfeld, Moshe. 1990. "The Common Heritage of Covenantal Traditions in the Ancient World." In *I Trattati nel mondo antico, forma, ideologia, funzione*. Edited by Luciano Canfora, Mario Liverani, and Carlo Zaccagnini. L'Erinna di Bretschneider. 17–191.

West, Martin L. 2011a. "Analysts." In *The Homer Encyclopedia*, Vol. 1. Edited byt Margalit Finkelberg. Wiley-Blackwell. 47–50.

2011b. "Unitarians." In *The Homer Encyclopedia*, Vol. 3. Edited by Margalit Finkelberg. Wiley-Blackwell. 911–913.

Whitehouse, Harvey. 2004. *Modes of Religiosity*. Altamira Press.

Willerslev, Rane, Piers Vitebsky, and Anatoly Alekseyev. 2015. "Sacrifice As the Ideal Hunt: A Cosmological Explanation for the Origin of Reindeer Domestication." *Journal of the Royal Anthropological Institute* 21(1):1–23. www.jstor.org/stable/43907808

Wilson, Donna. 2002. *Ransom, Revenge, and Heroic Identity in the* Iliad. Cambridge University Press.

Wintermute, Bobby. 2020. *Great War, Religious Dimensions*. Cambridge University Press.

Yates, Robin C. S. 2013. "Human Sacrifice and the Rituals of War in Early China." In *Sacrifices humains: Perspectives croisées et représentations* [online]. University Press of Liege. 153–173. https://doi.org/10.4000/books.pulg.8173

Yu, Jimmy. 2012. *Sanctity and Self-Inflicted Violence in Chinese Religions, 1500–1700*. Oxford University Press.

Zanker, Graham. 1994. *The Heart of Achilles*. University of Michigan Press.

Zeitlin, Froma I. 1965. "The Motif of the Corrupted Sacrifice in Aeschylus' Oresteia." *Transactions and Proceedings of the American Philological Association* 96:463–508.

  1966. "Postscript to Sacrificial Imagery in the Oresteia (Ag. 1235–37)." *Transactions and Proceedings of the American Philological Association* 97:645–653.

  1991. "Introduction." In *Mortals and Immortals: Collected Essays*. Edited by Jean-Pierre Vernant. Princeton University Press. 3–24.

Cambridge Elements ≡

Religion and Violence

James R. Lewis
Wuhan University

James R. Lewis is Professor at Wuhan University, and the author and editor of a number of volumes, including *The Cambridge Companion to Religion and Terrorism*.

Margo Kitts
Hawai`i Pacific University

Margo Kitts edits the *Journal of Religion and Violence* and is Professor and Coordinator of Religious Studies and East-West Classical Studies at Hawaii Pacific University in Honolulu.

ABOUT THE SERIES

Violence motivated by religious beliefs has become all too common in the years since the 9/11 attacks. Not surprisingly, interest in the topic of religion and violence has grown substantially since then. This Elements Series on Religion and Violence addresses this new, frontier topic in a series of ca. fifty individual Elements. Collectively, the volumes will examine a range of topics, including violence in major world religious traditions, theories of religion and violence, holy war, witch hunting, and human sacrifice, among others.

Cambridge Elements $\equiv$

Religion and Violence

Judaism and Violence: A Historical Analysis with Insights from Social Psychology
Robert Eisen

Violence in Pacific Islander Traditional Religions
Garry Trompf

Violence and the Sikhs
Arvind-Pal S. Mandair

Sacrifice: Themes, Theories, and Controversies
Margo Kitts

A full series listing is available at: www.cambridge.org/ERAV

Printed in the United States
by Baker & Taylor Publisher Services